MW01493115

ON THE EVOLUTION OF INTIMACY

Also by Charles Johnston:

The Creative Imperative: Human Growth and Planetary Evolution

Necessary Wisdom: Meeting the Challenge of a New Cultural Maturity

Pattern and Reality: A Brief Introduction to Creative Systems Theory

The Power of Diversity: An Introduction to the Creative Systems Personality Typology

An Evolutionary History of Music: Introducing Creative Systems Theory Through the Language of Sound (DVD)

Quick and Dirty Answers to the Biggest of Questions: Creative Systems Theory Explains What It Is All About (Really)

Cultural Maturity: A Guidebook for the Future

Hope and the Future: Confronting Today's Crisis of Purpose

Online:

The Institute for Creative Development: www.CreativeSystems.org

Creative Systems Theory: www.CSTHome.org

Cultural Maturity: www.CulturalMaturity.org

The Creative Systems Personality Typology: www.CSPTHome.org

An Evolutionary History of Music: www.Evolmusic.org

Cultural Maturity: A Blog for the Future: www.CulturalMaturityBlog.net

Looking To The Future podcast: www.LookingtotheFuture.net

ON THE EVOLUTION OF INTIMACY

A Brief Exploration
into the Past, Present, and Future
of Gender and Love

CHARLES M. JOHNSTON, MD

The Institute for Creative Development (ICD) Press
Seattle, Washington

The Institute for Creative Development (ICD) Press, Seattle, Washington

Cover design by Java Niscala

Author photo by Brad Kevelin

Library of Congress Control Number: 2019905436

First printing 2019

ON THE EVOLUTION OF INTIMACY

A World of Change

Nothing more defines gender and love today than change. Indeed, because these changes are so striking—and so far-reaching and fundamental in their implications—I often use them as examples of the broader changes that are reordering culture. This short book turns specifically to how changes in the worlds of gender and love are altering the human experience.

Two questions will be constant companions throughout these reflections. First, just how do we best understand the changes we see and interpret their effects? Some, such as greater gender equality, are obviously positive, while others, such as increasing divorce rates, can seem much less so. And second, just what do today's easily confusing new realities ask of us? What awarenesses, skills, and capacities will be needed if we are to successfully navigate realities that are likely to change even more dramatically in decades ahead?

The perspective I will draw on in addressing these questions is unusual. I'm a psychiatrist, and much in my observations will reflect my experience working hands-on with individuals and couples who are attempting to make their way in today's new gender and love landscape. But I'm also a futurist. Because of this, what I propose will as much come from understanding what we see today in the context of more encompassing cultural changes.

In addition, in contrast to what we commonly encounter with both popular and academic cultural commentary, I will engage these concerns from a very big-picture, long-term vantage. I will at times look back thousands of years. And in looking ahead, my concern will often be as much with what we are likely to encounter twenty, fifty, or a hundred years from now as with the changes we confront today.

That fact that I do so is of much more than just abstract interest. By the book's conclusion, it should be clear that we can understand gender and love at more than a surface level only with big-picture, long-term perspective. It should also be clear that big-picture, long-term perspective is necessary if we are to engage today's gender- and love-related conversations and controversies with the needed sophistication.

The book's conclusions will frequently be provocative and often controversial. A small handful provide a "preview of coming attractions":

1) I will describe how the ways we think about and experience love have evolved, and how they continue to evolve. And I will propose that our times challenge us to engage a new chapter in that evolution, one as significant in its newness as that which brought us Romeo and Juliet–style romantic love 300 years ago.

2) I will describe how, in similar ways, our thinking about identity has evolved and continues to evolve. And I will propose that changes happening today in how we think about identity are as fundamental in their significance as those that brought us the modern-age concept of the individual and modern institutions such as representative governance. Of particular significance for this inquiry, this includes changes in how we think about gender identity.

3) We will examine how, consistent with the fundamental nature of these changes, both love and identity are requiring skills and capacities new to us as a species. We will see how this is similarly the case whether our concern is authentic equality between the sexes, effectively honoring gender diversity, or learning to love in ways that can work going forward. Much of my reason for writing this book is a desire to help people understand and develop those needed new skills and capacities.

4) We will also examine further essential awarenesses that come from this new picture. For example, we will look at how our historical tendency to view men and women as polar opposites has had more to do with how our thinking processes have worked in times past than it does with the actual truth of the matter. We will also look at how a more big-picture perspective reveals gender-related insights that at first might seem paradoxical: We

come to see that men and women are more similar than we have assumed in times past. And, at the same time, we come to better appreciate real differences.

5) Throughout these reflections, I will observe how the tasks ahead challenge both men and women. These new tasks relate both to how men and women see themselves and how each views the other. For example, we will look at how men and women are equally capable of causing harm in relationships—in their own ways of being "violent." We will also look at how historical perspective brings into question commonly accepted conclusions about the roots of gender discrimination and conflict between the sexes, and how this perspective requires both men and women to take greater responsibility. And we will look too at how men and women in our time each tend to be disconnected from aspects of our complex natures that we need for really deep human relating. I will propose that the changes this book is about require a depth of engagement with that complexity that is only now becoming possible—indeed, that they follow naturally from it.

Another way this inquiry is unusual is in the conceptual approach that underlies its conclusions. To get the needed big-picture, long-term perspective, the book draws extensively on the ideas of Creative Systems Theory (CST), a comprehensive framework for understanding purpose, change, and interrelationship in human systems which was developed by myself and my colleagues at the Seattle-based Institute for Creative Development over the last forty years. CST views history as an evolutionary process that goes through identifiable "developmental" stages. Applying the theory to gender and love will let us step back and better appreciate these essential aspects of human experience in the larger context of culture's evolving story.

To bring detail to our understanding of the particular times in which we live, the book applies one specific CST notion. The concept of Cultural Maturity describes how our times are demanding (and making possible) a new chapter in our human narrative—put in developmental terms, an essential "growing up" as a species. We will look at how changes we see today in how we think about identity, gender, and love are natural consequences of this new cultural chapter.

For our task in these pages, the concept of Cultural Maturity will assist us in multiple ways. It will make understandable why we are seeing such fundamental changes in our time. (I will argue that it is hard to fully make sense of the changes currently reordering our experience of identity, gender, and love if something like what the concept of Cultural Maturity describes is not basically correct.) It will help clarify the new skills and capacities that will be needed if our love- and gender-related choices in times ahead are to be good ones. It will also help us grasp the changes in how we understand that will be necessary if needed new skills and capacities are to be realized and effectively put into practice. (I will argue that without Cultural Maturity's changes, it is hard to imagine deeply felt identity and successful love being possible in the future.)

Particularly when it comes to love, all this might seem like too much "thinking." We've tended in times past to view thinking and love as almost opposites. As we will see, given how we've before understood thinking and also how we've understood love, seeing them as not just opposites, but often as adversaries, has made perfect sense.

Two factors make the situation with this inquiry different. First is how identity and love today each require that we bring greater nuance and responsibility to our discernments. This does not mean being more analytical in making our choices—a major conclusion of CST is that addressing today's challenges requires more than just thought as we usually think of it. But it does mean that we need to make choices that better honor the uniqueness of who we are and the particulars of our circumstances.

The second factor pertains to just how the type of thought required to address these challenges is different. (Its importance should become increasingly clear as the book progresses.) CST's approach to understanding is unique in that it inherently draws on the whole of our cognitive complexity—always as much on the relational worlds of feelings and emotions, the inspired possibilities of imagination, and the sensory and sensual realities of the body as on the intellect. In so doing, it helps us think with greater detail about identity and love while at the same time taking us closer to them as direct experience. As a bonus, because these less conscious aspects of intelligence are exactly the parts of ourselves that we tend to be disconnected from in our time, drawing on CST's approach to understanding directly supports the new skills and capacities that the future of identity and love depend on.

A related way CST will serve us with this inquiry is reflected in the book's subtitle: A Brief Exploration Into the Past, Present, and Future of Gender and Love. A person would not expect such an exploration to be "brief." What allows me to keep this volume to only 160 pages is that CST gives as much attention to pattern as to particulars. The recognition of big-picture pattern will often allow us to capture complex dynamics with single-brushstroke succinctness.[1]

Is this book for everyone? If you ascribe to pretty traditional ideas of what it means to be a man or a woman and are comfortable with the picture of marriage and family broadly shared over the last century, what I describe may well be more than you wish to consider. You may also not be delighted with the book if you find political correctness a priority—whatever the particular flavor of socio-political correctness. Culturally mature perspective challenges us to address questions of all sorts in more encompassing and complete—more systemic—ways. As far as political correctness, it alerts us to how liberal and conservative (and also middle-of-the-road) ideological views, each in its own way not only fails to provide useful answers, more often than not they miss the real questions. This applies to ideological positions we might take with regard to gender and love as much as it does to more obviously ideological concerns.

My reference to how the book challenges both men and women provides good illustration. Women's issues—and with them, changes needed on the part of men—are today being given particular, and essential, new attention. I will applaud this. But I will also emphasize that while men obviously have much to learn from today's gender-related conversations, women do as well. Indeed, because the conversation right now, at least in liberal/progressive circles, tends to focus almost entirely on the blindnesses of men, I will often be particularly careful to be balanced in this regard.[2]

---

1 Besides being an exploration into identity, gender, and love, The Evolution of Intimacy can also be thought of as an examination of one particular application of Creative Systems Theory. As such, it can also be thought of as a test of the theory. To the degree the book provides helpful guidance, it serves as evidence for the theory's accuracy.

2 In my psychiatry practice, I frequently work with young men who find themselves rightfully confused by today's changing realities and often

ON THE EVOLUTION OF INTIMACY

Near the end of the book, I will turn specifically to contemporary conversations spawned by efforts such as the #MeToo movement.[3] I will describe how the general direction of such advocacy is almost wholly positive. But I will also propose that the larger part of what we have seen to this point is better understood as a culminating expression of the modern age project[4] than a reflection of Cultural Maturity's needed further changes. And I will emphasize that we can be vulnerable in these conversations to simplistic conclusions that in the end benefit neither women nor men. Over the course of the book, I will touch on a handful of complexities that we must keep in mind if such advocacy is ultimately to serve us.

By the book's conclusion, the reader should be able to bring more nuanced and sophisticated perspective to today's essential gender- and love-related conversations. The reader should also come to appreciate some of the great rewards that come with such perspective. For example, we will see how Cultural Maturity's changes should bring, with time, a lessening of "the battle of the sexes." I don't mean this in some utopian, idealized sense. Men and women will always at times have conflicting needs. But this lessening of the kind of conflict we have seen in the past is a result that follows naturally from Cultural Maturity's changes. If we can bring the needed complexity of perspective to today's gender- and love-related conversations, these conversations should support relegating at least the most egregious aspects of the battle of the sexes to history. If we can't, even if we are well intentioned, the result of these conversations could be the opposite. We could very well see the same kind of extreme, reactive polarization we witness today in the political sphere.

---

contradictory expectations. Being able to step back in a way that clarifies lessons to be learned all the way around proves particularly important for helping these young men make sense of changes being asked of them in our time and why they are important.

3 For those who are reading this book well after its initial date of publication, the #MeToo movement was an effort in the spring of 2018 to bring new attention to male abuse of power and sexual misconduct. It began with the highlighting of abusive behavior in Hollywood.

4 Which gave us the Bill of Rights and has produced increasing emphasis on equal rights and equal opportunity in centuries since.

This book comes at the challenge ahead for men and women from multiple directions, each of which interplays with the others. In the pages ahead, we will examine the roots of our experience of gender and love and how that experience has evolved through history. We will look more deeply at just what is new in today's new chapter in how we understand ourselves and connect with those we care about. We will tease apart some of the new skills and capacities we will need if identity and love are to work going forward. We will examine some of the particular tasks ahead for men and for women. And we will reflect on how these changes support new kinds of fulfillment as we look into the future.

Again, this book is not for everyone—at least not everyone right now. Depending on your life experience, it may be decades before the emerging realities examined here manifest in a major way in your life. If you are only beginning to be impacted by the kinds of changes this book is about, you may find the book's reflections at best only abstractly interesting. That said, I will argue that the demands and possibilities this book is about will in time be pertinent to everyone.[5]

---

5 People of non-heterosexual orientation or with relationships to gender other than binary should find the book's approach respectful and honoring of their experiences. But it is also the case that I most often make the point of reference traditional heterosexual identity and relationship. If I addressed multiple kinds of experience each step along the way, the book would pretty quickly cease to be a "brief" exploration—and would also quickly take me beyond where I have sufficient expertise. I've chosen to trust that readers can add the needed perspective when appropriate. Thus, for example, at the end of Chapter Five, I list "Specific Learnings for Men" and "Specific Learnings for Women." With each list, I make reference to the fact that being a man or being a woman can be experienced in multiple ways. But I've also trusted that people will be able to make necessary translations.

CHAPTER ONE

Making Sense of Today's Changes

What is changing with gender and love? Certainly we can identify general change themes over the last century. The clear gender roles and established moral codes of times past have given way to much greater flexibility and more options in the choices we make. Average family size has diminished markedly,[1] with a growing number of people choosing not to have children at all.[2] Divorce has become increasingly common to the point that "until death do us part" has become the exception. And not just gender in the sense of roles and accepted behaviors, but our ideas about what it fundamentally means to be a man or a woman, have become increasingly plural and fluid.

We've also witnessed explicit advocacy for change, starting with the woman's suffrage movement, and in 1920 in the U.S., the ratification of the Nineteenth Amendment to the Constitution. The 1960s and 70s gave us the "summer of love" with its celebration of the body and sexuality. The 70s and 80s produced modern feminism's call for equal rights and equal opportunity. The 90's brought new advocacy for gay rights, with gay marriage and gays in the military eventually gaining acceptance. With this century, we've seen increased support for people who do not easily fit into binary gender categories and a growing call for transgender rights. And more recently, we've witnessed important new attention given to abuse of power and sexual misconduct, most specifically in the workplace, but also more broadly.

---

1 Over 50 percent of American adults today are single.

2 Birth rates are decreasing throughout the industrialized world. Up until recently, the United States was the lone exception. With 2018 statistics, it joins ranks with the other countries.

Is all of this change for the good? There are people who would argue that it represents quite the opposite, that it reflects an erosion of
moral order, or worse, that civilization as a whole has entered a time
of decline. And even where changes appear beneficial, they have often
had disturbing consequences. The fact that marriage is not as once-
and-for-all as it once was is at least disruptive, and often the source
of considerable pain. And while the social movements I've described
have been largely positive in their ultimate effects, most too have been
accompanied by blindnesses. For example, the sexual revolution of the
60s and 70s brought important new freedoms, but when viewed from
the perspective of today, it is clear too that those freedoms were often
not accompanied by the new responsibilities that we now know must
accompany them.

At the least, the changes we confront today require that we leave
behind much that we have known. And often they present uncomfort-
able new uncertainties and ambiguities. But unsettling consequences
acknowledged, it seems clear that the larger portion of the gender- and
love-related changes I've described are ultimately positive. They point
toward greater freedom of choice, equality of opportunity, and acceptance of diverse ways of being. And today we see other changes of a
more everyday sort that turn out to be just as significant when we take
a moment to consider them. I think, for example, of how comfortably
young men and young women today interact just as friends, something
that was rare only a few decades ago. In the end, all these changes—
whether more dramatic or more everyday—benefit us.

We are left with the essential question of just why we see these
changes. People tend to think of social change in terms of organized
change movements or specific policies. The kinds of explanations I tend
to emphasize are more systemic—they recognize interplaying causal
factors. And as I've noted, they are very often also evolutionary—they
bring attention to the role of underlying "developmental" change
processes. Here I will give particular attention to how we can think of
current changes in the worlds of gender and love in terms of systemic
dynamics of a specifically developmental sort.

A couple of these developmental contributors to what we see
are familiar, or at least they tie to explanations we commonly
hear cited. The first presents no real challenge to culture's most

recent story. Much in contemporary changes can be thought of as a simple extension of the same modern-age impetus toward greater individual determination that produced democratic governance and the American Bill of Rights. Modern efforts toward greater gender equality make a good example.

Understanding the second requires that we think more conceptually, but it is ultimately straightforward. Important aspects of today's new freedoms can be thought of as expressions of postmodern sensibilities. Postmodern thought first appeared philosophically in the nineteenth century and has played a growing role in academia in recent decades. It brings a willingness to challenge absolutist assumptions of all sorts. It is reasonable that this would include traditional assumptions that we've had about gender and love.

But it turns out that neither a simple extension of modern-age achievements nor a postmodern challenging of past absolutes can ultimately explain what we see today. We need more if today's changes are to make full sense. And of particular importance, we need more if our explanations are to help us develop the new capacities and ways of understanding needed to effectively make our way in what will likely be an even more uncertain and easily overwhelming future.

The main focus in these pages will be a third developmental step: the new cultural chapter I referred to in the preface as Cultural Maturity. Making full sense of Cultural Maturity's implications requires that we think in ways that are new to most people. But as we will see, the further kind of change process the concept describes will be increasingly essential to a vital and fulfilling human future, and as we will explore specifically with this book, to a vital and fulfilling future for gender and love.

Loving as Whole People

Love makes a good place to begin understanding Cultural Maturity's role in what we see. The phenomenon we call love is becoming different today not just in the forms it takes, but in its nature as felt experience. Ultimately, the changes we see have to do with what makes something love at all. Our times are requiring us to bring more to the experience of love than has ever before been necessary—and more than we human beings have before now been capable of.

Over three decades ago, I wrote an article I titled "A New Meaning for Love."[3] No piece I've written since has been more often cited. A few paragraphs adapted from the introductory section of that article offer a hint at just what is changing and what makes these changes significant:

> "My reaction to the dilemma of a couple who came to me recently for therapy helps highlight these changes in love and its workings. The couple showed a high degree of sensitivity to each other and were accustomed to security and contentment in their relationship. But lately they had begun to argue. Resentment and fear were entering their connection.

> "When listening to the couple, I was surprised by what I felt in myself. I empathized with their pain, but I was also aware of feeling respect, fascination, even excitement in hearing what they had to say. Over time, I found myself thinking of their frustrations and pain less as expressions of personal failings than as products of the integrity the couple had brought to their relationship. They had begun to push into a new cultural frontier, and their fears seemed quite appropriate to the uncertainty inherent in the challenges the frontier presented. What is that frontier? Put simply, it is to love as whole people."

What I was responding to could not be more important. Throughout our most recent chapter in culture's story, intimate bonds have involved two people, each functioning as parts, coming together to create a whole. Our job with love has been to find our "better half." In its time, this two-halves-make-a-whole dynamic has provided a rich and effective kind of connecting.

My grandparents provide a good example of the beauty of this kind of bond when it is historically timely. They met in grade school and were inseparable throughout their lives. Their purpose in love was to complete each other. They succeeded to such an amazing degree in doing this—in being the mythic brave knight and fair princess for

---

3   *In Context*, March 1985

each other—that when one died, the other followed within months. The primary "organism" of their existence was quite literally the whole created from the two of them together.

But something different is being asked of us today. Increasingly we are being challenged to connect not as two halves, but as separate whole beings. Bonding as two halves is a difficult security to surrender, but increasingly we are finding that there is really no choice. When one part of us tries to make someone else our solution, another part quickly acts to undermine it. We find ourselves creating struggle, doing something to put the other off, anything to regain our embryonic yet critical connection with a new sort of completeness in ourselves. Increasingly it is possible to love only to the degree to which we can find ways to relate to another person while remaining fully ourselves.

For these changes to make complete sense, we need to step back for some big-picture historical perspective. The whole notion that love is something that changes can be hard for people to get their minds around. We tend to assume that love is an eternal notion—that love is love. And if we do recognize that our ideas about love have evolved, we are likely to assume that love as we have known it in our time represents a culminating ideal. But in fact, love as we have tended to think of it—romantic love—is a relatively recent cultural "invention"—a product of our Modern Age[4]—and, by all evidence, not an end point. Romantic love is appropriately celebrated. It has provided a powerful step forward in love's evolution—toward, among other things, greater authority in our lives. Previously, love's determinations were made by families or by a matchmaker. But there is no reason to expect romantic love to be the end of love's story.

An easily startling recognition implied in what I have described supports the importance of something more. The modern-age Romeo and Juliet ideal represents something quite different from what we have assumed it to be about. We've tended to think of romantic love as love based on individual choice. But while choice set against the constraints of family expectations is without question much of what makes Romeo

---

4 We idealized romantic love in the Middle Ages, but that was unrequited love—love held at a safe, abstract distance.

and Juliet a compelling tale, the modern age romantic ideal is not yet about individual choice in the sense of choosing as separate whole people.

A further recognition makes the need for something more even more clear and inescapably important. Love as we have known it necessarily involves distortion. With romantic love, the bond is created through the projection of parts of ourselves—I ascribe feminine aspects of myself to you; you ascribe masculine aspects of yourself to me. And as always happens with projection, we also mythologize the other, in this case making that person the magic answer to our lives (or, at less pleasant moments, the great cause of our suffering). Not only is romantic love not yet love between whole people, it is not yet love that reflects who the two people involved actually are.

The fact that love as we have witnessed it to this point has been based on projection becomes obvious with reflection. Projection is what makes it possible to fall quickly in love with no real knowledge of the other person. It is also what makes it possible for the sound of wedding bells at a movie's conclusion to assure us that the protagonists will live "happily ever after" when, in fact, love's journey has barely begun.

The common result when we fall out of love provides even more inescapable evidence. People tend to assume that we will then have distaste, even antipathy for the other person—which with high frequency is what we in fact feel. Notice that this outcome makes no sense if love had been between two whole people, if we have loved each other simply for who we are. The ending of such a relationship can bring significant sadness, but only in very unusual circumstances would antipathy be warranted. Why do we assume antipathy? When love involves projection, antipathy is needed in order to extract the projected part and regain our full sense of ourselves.

It is important to appreciate that up until very recently romantic love's projective mechanisms have served us. Much of the "glue" of relationship—the magnetism of love and the basis of commitment—has come from this giving away of key dimensions of ourselves to the other. Not only have these mechanisms benefited us, they have made love possible. Making the other our answer has shielded us from uncertainties and complexities that we could not before have tolerated.

But, like it or not, two-halves-make-a-whole relating is ceasing to work. In my work as a therapist, I increasingly find people seeking more complete kinds of connecting.

For lack of a better term, I call what intimate relationship becomes with this needed next chapter in intimacy's evolving story simply Whole-Person love.[5] Alternatively, we could also call it culturally mature love, or what love becomes when it takes expression from the whole of ourselves as systems. I don't see Whole-Person love as some luxury. I think the future of intimacy depends on our ability to realize this new and fuller kind of connecting.

Whole-Person love at once offers immense rewards and presents significant new demands. As far as rewards, it offers the possibility of a deeper sense of personal identity in relationship. And because it involves bringing more of ourselves to the experience of relationship, it also offers deeper and more reliable kinds of bonds and more fulfilling ways of being together. Whole-Person love makes it possible, really for the first time, to deeply love another person simply for who they are.

As far as demands, the new freedoms that come with Whole-Person love mean that we choose between options that are not as clear and obvious as in times past. In addition, such love requires that we know both ourselves and the person we are with more deeply. And of particular significance, Whole-Person love requires that we accept limits to what we can be for one another. The other person stops being our ultimate answer—and, similarly, we no longer get to be the ultimate answer for them. Love increasingly requires that we recognize how, as Lily Tomlin put it, "we are all in this alone."[6]

Fortunately, however great the demands, the rewards make today's new chapter in love's story more than worth the effort. It is also the case, as we will see, that we really have no choice. These are changes "whose time has come."

---

5 I will put the term "Whole-Person" in initial caps throughout the book to emphasize that what I am referring to is a specific CST notion. In Chapter Four, I will address how related language is often used with more humanistic or spiritual thinking. I will also delineate how the reference in each case is to something fundamentally different (and not ultimately new).

6 See Chapter Five for a closer look at love and limits.

Cultural Maturity's Needed "Growing Up" as a Species

I've emphasized that neither a simple extension of modern-age in-dividualism nor a postmodern questioning of past absolutes adequately explains the changes we see today. As it applies to love, this essential recognition follows directly from what I have just observed.

In describing romantic love, I noted that we have idealized it as love based on individual choice. But I also described how Whole-Person love requires us to be more complete in ourselves. It turns out that Cultural Maturity's changes fundamentally challenge individualism as we have thought about it. True individualism becomes possible only with Cultural Maturity's changes. If we limit ourselves to modern-age notions of the individual, our ideas about love leave us well short of what is being required of us today.[7]

Whole-Person love also involves a more complex result than we see with postmodern changes. Leaving behind familiar rules by itself would only leave us wandering aimlessly. Whole-Person love requires that we think in more complete and nuanced ways. In a fundamentally new sense, we must make our choices from the whole of who we are.

The concept of Cultural Maturity takes us beyond both modern-age beliefs and the newer sensibilities of postmodern perspective and provide explanation for what is most fundamental in today's needed new picture of identity and love. And the overarching vantage that becomes newly possible with culturally mature understanding provides perspective for making sense of gender-related changes that we have witnessed over the course of the last century.

Cultural Maturity involves two related change processes that are each today reordering the human experience. The first process concerns our relationship as individuals to culture as a whole. In every previous chapter in culture's evolving story, culture has functioned like a parent in the lives of individuals. It has provided us with our rules to live by, and in the process, our sense of connectedness, identity, and security. Cultural Maturity's "growing up" makes culture's parental function

---

7 CST has a formal term for modern-age beliefs about identity. The assump-tion that modernity has given us some final realization of identity is called The Myth of the Individual in CST. (See *Cultural Maturity: A Guidebook for the Future.*)

increasingly something of the past. CST proposes that it is this first step that produces what we call postmodern belief, with its absence of traditional guideposts.

The second process concerns basic changes in how we understand and hold experience. It provides an antidote to postmodern aimlessness. It also makes possible more Whole-Person kinds of relating. Cultural Maturity brings with it changes in ourselves—specific cognitive changes. Later we will look more closely at just what they involve.[8] For now it is enough to observe that these changes make it possible to more fully engage the whole of our cognitive complexity, and in the process the whole of ourselves.[9]

These changes fundamentally alter how we think about and experience identity. I find a basic image useful for beginning to grasp just how it does. Think of a box of crayons. The crayons, with their complex array of hues, represent our various psychological parts. The box represents the ability to hold that complexity. Whole-Person identity is what we get when we successfully do so.

In a related way, these changes redefine relationship. Using our box of crayons metaphor, with two-halves-make-a-whole relationship, crayons in one person relate to crayons in another. And that is only part of it. More accurately, crayons in one person relate to images of crayons of an opposite sort that are projected onto the other person. The result is an illusion of completion when in fact the other person is barely involved. With Whole-Person relationship, each person celebrates their own whole-box-of-crayons completeness and connects with the other person from it.

Later we will see how the way that Cultural Maturity's cognitive changes alter identity and love also has essential implications for how

---

8 See Chapters Three and Four.

9 These cognitive changes have implications for more than just the projective dynamics that have given us our modern pictures of gender and love. They are equally pertinent to thinking of any sort that we have before framed in the language of polarity—from relegating thoughts and feelings or mind and body to wholly separate worlds to our past need to divide our collective social realities into "chosen people" and "evil others." See in particular my early book, *Necessary Wisdom: Meeting the Challenge of a New Cultural Maturity*.

we think about gender. Our ideas about gender, like those we have had about identity and love, have been based on projection. Because of this, not only have they been incomplete, they have also necessarily involved distortion.

Again, as I've described for love, the fact that our beliefs about gender have been based on projection is not in itself a problem. We will look at how our ideas about what it means to be a man or a woman have been predictably different at different times in history and how our beliefs at particular times have served the needs of those times. But appreciating underlying dynamics helps us make sense of why we have had some of the beliefs we've had. It also offers us a chance to begin to understand gender in fuller ways.

Bringing evolutionary perspective to how we think about gender can also help us rethink relationships between the sexes. In later chapters, we will look at how Cultural Maturity's changes help us get beyond projections that previously have gotten in the way of our seeing one another simply as people. We will also examine how they help us more deeply get in touch with what it means to be embodied, and through this, what might be particular in any person's experience of gender.

It would be easy to think of Whole-Person love and Whole-Person identity mostly as dreams of some far-off future. But the fact that I wrote about these changes years ago suggests otherwise. And if some of the other gender- and love-related changes noted earlier have related origins, we have added evidence that these changes are well underway. That said, it is also very much the case that we are only just beginning to see the full expression of these new realities. Certainly Hollywood depictions rarely get beyond two-halves-make-a-whole love of the most trivial sort and only hint at how deeply identity is in flux. But I believe these changes describe what will increasingly—and necessarily—define identity and love over the next century. If identity and love are to work in times ahead, venturing into this new, more mature territory of experience becomes essential.

Personal Reflections

Some reflections from my personal experiences as a young man trying to make sense of gender and love help set the stage for later reflections. I offer them because they provide further insight into just what is becoming different and also because they point toward some important surprises with regard to how we have ended up with today's gender-related expectations.

To a degree rare for the times, in my family there was little emphasis on traditional gender roles. This was not because my parents were particularly enlightened socially, though they were more aware than most. It was more a simple product of circumstances, of who made up my childhood world.

One of these circumstances was the fact that the most significant people in my growing up were artists and musicians, a roughly equal number of them men and women.[10] My sister and I each had artistic interests, hers more in music and mine most in the visual arts, particularly sculpture. We each learned skills that might have been thought of as more masculine or more feminine. For example, as an opera singer she learned to project and have a strong stage presence. As a sculptor, among other things, I learned to sew, for the simple reason that a sewing machine is a tool that can be handy for sculptural endeavors.

Another circumstance was just as important. I had girl cousins of my age living next door. When the neighborhood crowd got together to play, we all played together. For both of these reasons, throughout my early years, while I was attracted to girls sexually, I didn't think of them as that different from myself. For the most part I didn't see any reason to treat them differently from my other friends.

But that changed quickly when I entered school. Other kids, both boys and girls, had had more conventional upbringings with clearer gender expectations. Suddenly guys began talking about girls as if they were a different species. And very often the girls were in fact behaving like a different species.

In particular, there were surprises with how boys and girls were supposed to act if they had interest in one another. For example, it was

---

10 In Chapter Six I will describe how the personality styles of people most likely to become artists make them particularly open to a more encompassing and accepting picture of gender. Historically, there has been significant discrimination against women in the arts, but at least in my world growing up, male and female artists most often treated one another with respect.

clear that the guy was supposed to do the initiating and pursuing,[11] and that the girl, at least initially, was expected to not really let on if she had interest—to, at least a bit, play hard to get.

There was also a further, less-than-pleasant surprise. It turned out that very often girls were less interested in generally nice guys like myself who could be friends than in guys of the more "bad boy" sort.[12]

I remember talking with my male friends about how all that seemed unnecessarily complicated and a bit absurd. But we concluded that this must just be how things worked and that we would need to learn to play the game.

The polarized picture became even more extreme with college and formal dating. There was then a mostly unverbalized assumption that young men and young women were supposed to be magnetic opposites. When it came to love, my task was to find a magic other who could complete me—who could be my other half—and in turn to be this kind of magical completion for the other person.

I'm struck now by how much in my learnings about gender and love that came with decades since has involved challenging beliefs I acquired during those school years. I'm struck too by how much in at least my initial rethinking was implied in what had just seemed reasonable when I was younger.

Such rethinking began with questioning the value of conventional role expectations. It came to make less and less sense to me, for example, that it was my job as a man to always be protector and provider (though I was happy to be a bit of either at times, depending on the circumstances). Similarly, I questioned whether the woman should be expected to be always either nurturer or cheerleader (though at times a bit of one or the other could be nice). At a deeper level, I questioned the whole idea that someone else should be my answer and completion.

---

11 If one has doubts about this being the conventional expectation, think of how Sadie Hawkins Day, a day when the girls get to chase the boys (invented by Li'l Abner cartoonist Al Capp), would not have been needed if the opposite arrangement was not assumed for the other days of the year.

12 By "bad boy" I don't necessarily mean troublemaker. It could also be the sports star or the son of wealthy parents. The common denominator was that these were guys who would not be inclined to take no for an answer.

The notion seemed increasingly to get in the way of love, at least love that could work for me.

With time, I found myself reflecting more specifically on what here I refer to as Whole-Person identity and love. I found growing fascination with trying to understand what bringing greater completeness to identity and love might look like. And I found myself more and more intrigued with the greater possibility it seemed to imply.

None of these gender- and love-related learnings made love—or life—easier. And the needed stretching has not stopped. For example, parts of me can at times still find it difficult to leave behind that magical hope that there is someone who might know me completely. But gradually it has become obvious that not only is it not a woman's job to know me completely and mine similarly to completely know her, the whole notion that anything close to this is possible is absurd. Over time, I've come to appreciate that it can only be in our mutual completeness that the kind of love that I would want—love that could really add to my life—might be possible.

Complexity and Simplicity—
Paradox and a New Common Sense

Whole-Person identity and Whole-Person love each propel us into more complex and often uncertain worlds. That they do should not take us by surprise. A main function of cultural dictates such as gender roles has been to protect us from complexity and uncertainty. Gender roles have provided one-size-fits-all rules for making our way amongst the endless ways we can be different. And the reliable magnetisms that come with projection and polarization in a similar way have protected us from doubt and any real need to understand nuance. Like it or not, Whole-Person identity and love challenge us to engage realities that are complex, uncertain, and demanding in ways that before now would have overwhelmed us.

Fortunately for any likelihood of success with the tasks ahead, this more complex and demanding picture also brings with it what might seem a paradox. There are important ways in which Cultural Maturity's changes make identity and love simpler. Without this result, I don't think taking on all that this new picture asks would be possible. It follows naturally from what we see if we step back and consider what makes Whole-Person identity and Whole-Person love different from what we have known.

With Cultural Maturity's changes, we begin to see how a major part of the experiences we have called life and love—both what has made them exciting and what has made them so often difficult—has had more to do with what we lay on top of them as experience than what they are ultimately about. When we recognize this fact, there are essential ways in which reality becomes more straightforward. In the end, Whole-Person identity and love are about simply being in the world honestly and taking responsibility in doing so. They are about making good choices and stating our yeses and nos clearly and with integrity. Ultimately, the rules of Whole-Person love are not that different from those that we rely on with the best of friendships (and not that different from what it means to be the best friend one can be with oneself).[13] I think of this easily contradictory-seeming outcome as part of a "new common sense" that is only just now becoming possible to grasp.

Other recognitions that are important for today's new picture of identity and love similarly reflect this at once more complex and simpler kind of common sense. One recognition of particular importance concerns how we best think about the realities of times past. It reflects a kind of shift that comes with bringing culturally mature perspective to any kind of question. I've proposed that the two-halves-make-a-whole picture of identity and love that culturally mature perspective challenges was right for its time, and thus is not a problem. It becomes a problem only if we continue to hold onto it going forward. Developmental perspective makes the past not wrong, but simply no longer timely.

Another such new-common-sense recognition is related and ultimately just as important. We see that no one is to blame for the teaching of roles and ways of relating that today cease to serve us. When they were timely, they were taught by the social system as a whole. We can miss this. For example, people today are likely to ascribe male behaviors that can no longer work to the teachings of parents or social pressure from other boys. Note that in my case, expected behavior toward

---

13 It should be noted that culturally mature friendship ultimately requires the same leap as culturally mature love. At the least, it stops being about always being on someone else's side.

girls was at least as much communicated by the behavior of the girls. The love- and gender-related assumptions of any time are aspects of larger realities of which we are all a part and from which we all benefit (and for which we all also pay the price).

A further essential way that Cultural Maturity results in greater simplicity (as long as we can tolerate the complexity) involves how it has the potential to bring a marked lessening of conflict and drama. A certain amount of conflict is an inevitable consequence of the fact that two people are going to have different needs. But the larger portion of conflict of the drama sort is a product of failing at two-halves-make-a whole relationship tasks—such as being the other person's answer and understanding them completely. It is a product of one person's "crayons" sparring with the "crayons" of another. Conflict of the drama variety stops serving any purpose when a person begins to become capable of Whole-Person relationship.

One of the best places to see this essential difference brings us back to my earlier observations about what tends to happen when a love relationship ends. I described how love relationships based on romantic projection tend not to end pleasantly. The reason is not hard to understand from what I have described. Separation requires that we extract the projected parts of ourselves. Often we create the needed distance by replacing the idealized projections that drew us together with projections of an "evil other" sort.

I've suggested that Whole-Person love relationships tend to end differently. There can be significant disappointment and sadness that things no longer work as they have, and deep grieving at the loss. There can also be regrets that mistakes were made. But at the least, there tends to be gratitude for what was shared even if ultimate dreams could not be fulfilled. Often people remain friends in some way.

Notice that this result is again rather common sense. If we were initially attracted to someone and we have any capacity for good judgment, he or she was probably a good person. And if we stayed in the relationship with that person over time, he or she was probably basically good for us. That the person might be now seen as evil, if this conclusion has any basis in fact, can only reflect our own failings (that we could have chosen to be with—and stay with—such an evil person).

In later chapters, I will describe how this getting beyond ultimately unhelpful—and unnecessary—conflict and drama extends beyond the personal to gender's big picture. I will propose that much of what we have witnessed historically as conflict between the sexes has been a product of ways we have protected ourselves from realities that before now would have been more than we could handle.

The new, and newly demanding, kind of common sense our future requires of us asks a lot. It can overwhelm us. But if we can tolerate all it asks, the result is an ultimately more caring picture in which much more becomes possible.

CHAPTER TWO

The Roots of Gender Identity

I've proposed that love in the future will require us to think more deeply about love's workings than has been necessary in times past. I've also proposed that we need to think more deeply about identity, including gender identity. There are ways in which thinking deeply about identity is not at all new—it is what philosophers have done for centuries, and it is the stock-in-trade of psychologists. But as we shall see, with gender, as with love, in the end the task is not just to think more deeply, but to think in some fundamentally new ways.

We've made a start. I've pointed toward how the polarized perceptions of times past have resulted in distorted pictures of gender and gender differences. And later I will take such observations considerably further. In Chapter Four, we will look at how the way cultural systems evolve lets us both understand why we have viewed gender in the polarized ways we have and why at different times those polarized interpretations have taken the various forms we have seen.

With this chapter, I introduce a way of thinking that will provide both essential beginning insights and a foundation for these later, more in-depth reflections. Of particular significance for this inquiry, the approach we will draw on lets us begin to address a question that becomes obviously important once we recognize that the polarized perceptions of times past are not enough: Just how are men and women in fact different? Just what are we left with when we step beyond the mythologized projections of times past?

Certainly there are biological differences, and by virtue of particular biology-specific activities we engage in, such as bearing children, we may have different life experiences. But my question has more to do with what we might conventionally think of as psychological differences.

Are men and women different in terms of values, attitudes, beliefs, and emotional responses? I've suggested that men and women are much less natively different than we tend to assume. But just as important is recognizing real differences. These are differences of a normative sort—there is great variation between individuals. But making sense of such differences provides valuable insight.

The simple observation that we find normative differences between men and women can be controversial. Contemporary academic thought, with its postmodern learnings, can claim that psychological differences, if they exist at all, are products only of conditioning, of the different ways boys and girls are raised. Indeed, it is possible in academia today to lose one's job simply for suggesting the existence of differences of a more fundamental sort. But the fact of differences seems obvious to most people. Most people who spend much time around young children, for example, would not find at all persuasive the conclusion that all we need is upbringing to explain apparent differences.

The more systemic vantage I will draw on here helps us appreciate such differences and their implications. In the process, it will also help us appreciate why more simplistic ways of thinking about identity and gender—whether the polarized assumptions of times past or some postmodern unisex ideal—inevitably leave us short. In addition, it will provide important preparation for addressing how our experience of differences has evolved over the course of history and teasing apart specific challenges that men and women confront in our times.

Gender Archetype

The concept of gender archetype provides the basic language for the approach we will draw on. The notion has been best articulated in modern times by psychiatrist Carl Jung and will be familiar to many people with a psychological background. Jung proposed that we each have more masculine and more feminine aspects and described how we see the workings of these counterpoised forces in fairy tales, in myth, and also in spiritual practices and philosophical thought.[1]

---

1 Jung called the feminine in a man the "anima," and the masculine in a woman the "animus."

In Chapter Four, we will examine how CST invites us to think more complexly not just about how these forces interplay, but also about why we might see them in the first place. For now, I will observe simply that we can usefully think of some of the "crayons" in the systemic box I described in the previous chapter as more "archetypally masculine," and others as more "archetypally feminine."

I include the somewhat clumsy adjective "archetypal" in describing these qualities to avoid confusing tendencies in this sense with the common assumption that some qualities are male and others female. Again, men and women each embody both kinds of tendency. A man or a woman might have more archetypally masculine or more archetypally feminine characteristics regardless of their gender, depending on their personality style, The balance in a man may be more archetypally feminine than in the average woman, and that in a woman more archetypally masculine than in the average man. In Chapter Six, we will examine not just how this is the case, but why this can be what we find.

There are simpler ways to talk about what I am here calling archetypally masculine and archetypally feminine. For example, I often speak of more "right-hand" and more "left-hand" psychological aspects. We could also use more everyday language and talk about qualities that are "harder" or "softer." But the language of gender archetype, besides helping us think with particular nuance about difference, also points toward essential conceptual insights. Later I will describe how it highlights the important recognition that there is something inherently "procreative" in how polar opposites relate (and ultimately in how human intelligence is structured).

To bring needed nuance to our examination of archetypally masculine and archetypally feminine tendencies, we need to start with an observation I first made in my 1984 book *The Creative Imperative*. We can think of these tendencies as having both "horizontal" and "vertical" aspects.[2] Horizontal aspects are more interpersonal. We can think of them as contrasting more expressive (archetypally masculine) and more receptive (archetypally feminine) dimensions of experience. Ver-

---

2 CST delineates how these tendencies reflect not just psychological attributes, but also different aspects of bodily experience.

tical aspects have more to do with how we relate to ourselves, both as individuals and as social systems. More vertical archetypally masculine aspects emphasize ascent—preeminence and standing tall. More vertical archetypally feminine aspects address the ground of being, both in its foundational and more generative dimensions.

CST uses the simple terms Upper Pole and Lower Pole to describe the archetypally masculine and archetypally feminine dimensions of the vertical. It speaks of Outer and Inner creative aspects to refer to the archetypally masculine and archetypally feminine dimensions of the horizontal.

Drawing on this more filled-out picture of gender archetype will take us a long way toward understanding gender and gender differences in the more complete ways our times require. Such understanding starts with a recognition that follows directly from the fact of projection. The polarized perceptions of times past have had us confuse gender with gender archetype. It continues with the recognition that the particular forms such polarized perceptions have taken, whether they manifest in more vertical or more horizontal ways, have followed predictably from how culture has evolved.

One gender archetype–related observation is particularly important to note in getting started. It provides essential insight for understanding both current circumstances and challenges ahead for us as a species. In our time, we find it much easier to understand archetypally masculine qualities than we do qualities of a more archetypally feminine sort— whether more horizontal or more vertical.

For example, today we commonly confuse the receptive with simply being passive. In fact, the receptive, when experienced deeply, is fully as active—in the sense of being dynamic and creative—as is the expressive. And while we don't have a problem understanding the role of standing tall in authority, my reference to "the ground of being" as an equally important aspect of the vertical, even with explanation, might still seem obscure, and even a bit mysterious. Later we will look at how we find just the opposite to be the case if we go back far enough in history. With culture's beginnings, the archetypally feminine played the more defining role, and while still by its nature less explicit, got much the greater attention.[3]

---

3 Psychiatrist Jean Baker Miller, in her classic work *Toward a New Psychology*

But I am getting ahead of myself. We need first to engage the necessary preliminary step of better understanding gender archetype as I will be using the term. The brief descriptions that follow give voice to archetypally masculine and feminine gender archetypes in their various more vertical and horizontal manifestations.

With these descriptions, I've often drawn directly on observations from *The Creative Imperative*. I've done so only in part because that is where I've addressed the archetypally masculine and the archetypally feminine most specifically in my work. It is also because I chose to write *The Creative Imperative* with a style that consciously gave equal emphasis to the archetypally masculine and the archetypally feminine. The book can be thought of as equal parts prose and poetry. In crafting it, I attempted to draw with equal measure on the more rational aspects of intelligence that best give voice to the archetypally masculine and the less visible, more imaginal, emotional, and bodily aspects of intelligence that better voice the archetypally feminine (and which we are less used to associating with observations of a "theoretical" sort). Each description below includes a few quotations followed by some introductory reflections, each adapted from *The Creative Imperative*.[4]

The Horizontal—Archetypally Masculine Manifestations

Aspects that are more horizontal come alive in relationships with others. The archetypally masculine manifests here in expressive dynamics—in the thrust of a sword, in a well-chosen word, in a song sung powerfully. When we use words like "assertive" or "confrontative" we are referring to this aspect of the archetypally masculine.

---

of *Women*, wrote about how the qualities natively strongest in the psychology of women can today be difficult for people, including women, to consciously access and affirm. "Thus there is a dilemma. This abundance of women's psychological strengths exists but cannot flourish or come forward fully into a world that sorely needs precisely these kinds of strengths. And women themselves cannot really believe in them, give them credence, and draw on them as a basis for their development and growth.... Some women writers implicitly accept the model of the man as the only model of a seemingly full-fledged person." (See Jean Baker Miller, *Toward a New Psychology of Women*, 1976, Beacon Press, Boston, p.x.)

4 Sections drawn from *The Creative Imperative* are in quotes.

A few quotes that reflect this aspect:

Three kinds of prayers: I am a bow in your hands, Lord,
Draw me lest I rot.
Do not overdraw me, Lord, I shall break.
Overdraw me, Lord, and who cares if I break.
                                        —Nikos Kazantzakis

But such is the irresistible nature of truth, that all it asks, and all it wants,
is the liberty of appearing.
                                        —Thomas Paine

When I am a man then I shall be a hunter.
When I am a man then I shall be a harpooner.
When I am a man then I shall be a canoe-builder.
When I am a man then I shall be a carpenter.
When I am a man then I shall be an artisan.
Oh father! ya hahaha.
                                        —A Kwakiutl song

"Who are we as the expressive? Much of it is quite 'straightforward.' Our concern is with acting and doing. Myth offers us some good beginning images. The expressive embodies symbolically as the hero, and specifically as the hero's more active aspect. This active aspect can personify in an infinity of forms—the warrior, the poet, the inventor, the magician—but the essential quality is quite specific: the capacity to penetrate reality.

"Our colloquial language is rich with figures of speech that depict the expressive. Some simply describe movement outward, or how movement outward engages another's reality. We speak of 'getting through to someone,' of 'making a point' or 'an impression,' of 'getting something across,' or 'speaking out.' Others emphasize the finality intrinsic to expression: we 'put our cards on the table.' Many such figures of speech give voice to the inherent vulnerability of expression. We speak of 'going out on a limb,' or of 'putting ourselves on the line.'"

The forms expression takes can be subtle, as can what expression requires to manifest. A favorite quote from Cooper Eden's children's book *Remember the Night Rainbow* counsels us that "If your heart catches in your throat ... ask a bird how she sings." It is also the case that expression is ultimately more than just a matter of choice. The Gnostic Gospels remind us that "If you bring forth what is within you, what you bring forth will save you. If you do not bring forth what is within you, what you do not bring forth will destroy you." (*Gospel of Thomas*, 14.29-33)

The Horizontal—Archetypally Feminine Manifestations

Horizontally, the archetypally feminine manifests in receptive dynamics: in acts not just of listening but of hearing, in being aroused by or moved by, in aesthetic perception. When we see someone "taking in" experience or offering "invitation," we are witnessing the receptive. As with the horizontal aspect of the archetypally masculine, this complementary horizontal aspect of the archetypally feminine similarly often comes most alive in relationships with others.

A few quotes that give this aspect voice:

The sound of the gates opening wakes the beautiful woman asleep.
                                                    —Kabir (trans. Robert Bly)

Learning to draw is really a matter of learning to see and that means a good deal more than merely looking with the eye.
                                                    —Kimon Nicolaides

And then I asked him with my eyes to ask again yes
and then he asked me would I yes ...
and first I put my arms around him yes
and I drew him down to me so he could feel my breasts all
*   perfume yes*
and his heart going like mad
and yes I said yes I will yes.

                                                    —James Joyce

"Since it won't be possible to define the receptive by 'making a point,' I'll draw on a couple of images. The first comes from the legend of King Arthur. With his sword broken in battle, Arthur is led by Merlin to the shore of a small body of water. In it lives the beautiful Lady of the Lake. From her, Arthur receives the mighty sword Excalibur, with which he will found the great Round Table, and its scabbard. The sword is broad and sharp, embellished in gold. Engraved on one side are the words 'take me,' on the other, 'cast me away.'

"Standing before him, Merlin asks Arthur which he likes better, the sword or the scabbard. The sword is Arthur's quick choice. To this Merlin responds, 'In that you are unwise. Excalibur is a good sword, the best in the world. But the scabbard is worth far more. For however sorely you are beset in battle, you will not lose a drop of blood as long as you have the scabbard with you ....'

"The second image is from the beloved European folktale of Beauty and the Beast. We engage the story as Beauty, having run many hours through the entangled forest, finds the Beast outside his castle, his breath gone, the spell having done its evil work. Through her tears, moved by the love that has grown within, she embraces his terrible image. At that moment, the interminable spell that has imprisoned the prince is broken ...."

It can be easiest to make reference to this aspect of our power by saying what it is not, or by suggesting it indirectly. We frequently use sensory metaphors, though the five senses may not literally be central. We may say we "got a taste" of or "drank in" an experience, that we "saw" what someone was saying, or that we were "touched" or "moved" by the depth of a person's response. Frequently our words reflect the surrender of control intrinsic to the receptive moment. We speak of being amazed (from the same root as "maze") or being "taken" by an experience. Our words may reflect the letting down of boundaries, a recognition that we had let ourselves be "open," or that another person had "gotten through to us." Or they may describe our bodily experience when we do, such as feelings of warmth and responsiveness, or of being "turned on."

What is it we derive from the receptive? If the "purpose" of the expressive is to actively have an effect, how might we best describe that of the receptive? Perhaps the simplest way to say it is that our receptivity is the way we derive our human sustenance. We are fed by each aspect of real contact that we allow. When our "diet" is appropriate and sufficient, our life feels "full;" when it is not, we hunger.

To receive is always a vulnerable thing. We are inviting another to enter a room in our psychic house, knowing that with this visit, the room will never again be quite the same. And there is no guarantee that what is offered by the visitor will be positive. It could be that this visitor comes on false pretenses, intending only to rob or violate. As with expression, receptivity is always in the end a leap into the unknown. Ultimately, we can never be sure what the effect of an act of receiving will be until we have risked it. Yet how fully alive we are is precisely a function of how deeply we can engage doing so.

It is important to appreciate how deeply this aspect of who we are can confuse and elude us. By its nature the receptive is invisible—often we know it is there only by what becomes visible in its presence. It is an elusiveness dramatically amplified in our time by how distanced most people are today from receptive sensibilities.[5]

Yet, ultimately, the receptive is just as much a reflection of power as the expressive. Indeed, in many circumstances it is where the greater power lies. The Chinese sage Lao Tzu reminds us that "The softest thing in the universe overcomes the hardest thing in the universe." And as with the expressive, there is an important sense in which the receptive is more than just a matter of choice. I like these words from John Stuart Mill: "We must neglect nothing that could give the truth a chance to reach us."

The Vertical—Archetypally Masculine Manifestations

To fully grasp the archetypally masculine and the archetypally feminine, we also need to include their more vertical manifestations. In the vertical, the archetypally masculine manifests in the dynamics of ascent: think of the crown on the head of a king or queen, the crafting of an abstract idea, the construction of a great building, or a rocket headed into space. When we stand and take ownership in our lives we are giving emphasis to the ascendant aspect of experience. Ascent is about the power of above as opposed to the power of below.

---

5 We find last faint remnants of the receptive today in activities that involve consuming—such as buying things, eating (increasingly today to the point of obesity), and social media (often today to the point of addiction).

A few quotes that give this aspect voice:

In each of us there is a king; speak to him and he will come forth.
                                                    —A Norse Saying

[A new theory] is rather like climbing a mountain, gaining new and wider views, discovering new unexpected connection between our starting point and its rich environment.
                                                    —Albert Einstein

Form acts the father:
tells you what you may and
may not do.

                                                    —Theodore Roethke

"What is it that each new ascendant impulse offers that was not there before? First, ascent gives us perspective. With it, we rise above, find a place that allows us to see the forest where before we could see only trees. Second, it gives new form and substance to our reality. To ascend is at once to climb a mountain, and to be creating that mountain. Each new act of standing tall offers a leap in monumentality and complexity. And third, it offers us authority and autonomy. To grow up is to define our natures as distinct.

"Our cultural images for ascent and the ascendant trace a proud and dramatic lineage: the primitive's great bird of the spirit; the Greek sun god Helios or Apollo, driving each day across the heavens in a chariot with four great horses; Odin, wise and omnipotent, sitting on his throne in the upper branches of Yggdrasil (an eagle beside him, a crown on his head); the mountain as home of the divine—Qaf, Olympus, Sinai; the word as God; the uplifting spire of a European cathedral, Middle Eastern mosque, or Asian stupa; the firmament of heaven; the lifted transept of the Latin cross; the nation as flag; Washington, Napoleon, Churchill; Newton's laws of motion; the Bill of Rights; the Empire State Building; the first human walking on the surface of the moon."

Key recognitions about ascent are essential to fully grasping its significance. William Blake emphasized the close relationship between ascent and awareness with these words: "Awake, Awake, O sleeper of the land of shadows, awake." There is also how ascent is inseparable from responsibility. I think of these reflections from Martin Buber: "He has stepped out of the glowing darkness of chaos into the cool light of creation. But he does not possess it yet: he must first draw it truly out, he must make it into a reality for himself, he must find his own world by seeing, hearing, touching, and shaping it." And as with other aspects, ascent is not simply a matter of choice. A traditional song of the Bahamas announces: "Oh children, no grave could've keep that body down. Ain't no grave gonna keep that body down. When the trumpet sound ...."

The Vertical—Archetypally Feminine Manifestations

As with the receptive in the horizontal, the archetypally feminine aspect of the vertical confronts us with dimensions of our human power that are less explicit, and also less easily recognized in our time, indeed easily missed entirely. And, again, they are essential. In the ground of being, we find nurturance and sustenance and also the germinal beginnings of things. In addition, we find what, in our learning to stand tall, gives us something to stand upon.

Vertical aspects of the archetypally feminine manifest in our connectedness with nature, in religious imagery such as that of the Madonna holding the Christ child, and in the body's contribution both as the starting point of life's erotic impulses and the foundation of our being. In Chapter Four, we will see how the way we experience the ground of our being, as with each polar tendency, is not a single thing, but an evolving dynamic that takes us through a sequence of markedly different experiential realities.

A few quotes that reflect this aspect:

The land is a mother that never dies.

—A Maori saying

All matter is created out of some imperceptible substratum .. nothingness, unimaginable, and undetectable. But it is a particular form of nothingness out of which all matter is created.

—Physicist Paul Dirac

The spirit of the valley ... is called the mysterious female,
The fate of the mysterious female
   is called the root of heaven and earth,
Dimly visible, it seems as if it were scarcely there,
Yet use will never drain it.

— Lao Tzu

"In the 'ground' of our being, we find the power of mystery. Through our relationship with it, we experience the fact of our generativity and the 'foundation' of our existence. When this relationship is right and timely, it imbues life with such qualities as belonging, playfulness, rootedness, passion, and compassion.

"In the earliest stages in any creative process, this 'nothing' that is at once something is reality's predominant force. Here we encounter a secret shared by the very old and the very young. It is the place into which we die and from which we are born. It is from here that we know the eternal magic of things. In ancient Celtic myth it is the Ti-nan-og, the place that existed before the beginning of time. Winter rituals often pay homage to its deep mysteries."

The lower pole of the vertical is also where we find the erotic. This is so equally in men and in women. It is also where we find deep connection in nature. The erotic and the wild are key to who we are. And at the same time, encountering them may not be comfortable. They are always as much about destruction as creation.

An additional recognition that we will explore in detail in Chapter Four is important to making sense of developmental processes and also to grasping cultural dynamics that can easily be misunderstood. At a certain point in any creative process, we necessarily push away from this part of ourselves. This is equally so if our creative concern is a simple creative act like writing a book, individual development over the course of a lifetime, or the evolution of culture. Greek philosopher Ostanes described the progression this way: "Nature rejoices in nature. Nature subdues nature. Nature rules over nature." At the very least, we lose conscious contact with much of the potency of this part of ourselves. A Jewish saying observes that "in the mother's body, man knows the universe, in life he forgets it."

Later, we will see how this pushing-away dynamic provides explanation for how difficult it can be to make sense of the archetypally feminine in our time. It also helps us make sense of some of the less-than-positive ways men and women have viewed each other, and acted toward each other, at different times in history.

Archetype and Gender

Most immediately this look at experience through the lens of gender archetype helps highlight the richness and fecundity of human experience. But as I've suggested, these at once theoretical and poetic reflections also help us with the question of gender differences.

We gain initial insight by recognizing that gender archetypes have served as the templates for our polarized concepts of gender. In projecting, it has been gender archetypes that we projected. This recognition helps clarify an earlier observation critical to making sense of the absolutist gender beliefs of times past. I've proposed that historically we've confused gender with gender archetype. More precisely, our concepts of gender have been based on projected idealized/mythologized archetypal images and qualities. In Chapter Four, we will look at how our beliefs about gender differences through time have reflected the particular ways that gender archetype has manifested and been projected at specific points in the evolution of culture.

That helps us with history. But we are left with making sense of just what we find when we step beyond the past's projections and mythologizings. Just how does our picture of gender and gender differences change with culturally mature perspective?

I've touched previously on one part of the answer. With culturally mature perspective, we are better able to recognize how men and women each embody both archetypally masculine and archetypally feminine characteristics. Using our box-of-crayons image, with Whole-Person identity we better appreciate how men and women each have both archetypally masculine and feminine aspects.

This recognition might easily have us question whether there really are differences. If we are each composed of the same basic ingredients, wouldn't we then be essentially the same? But when we look closely, this is not what we find. The result is obviously more nuanced.

At the least we still live in different kinds of bodies. Given how the different-strokes-for-different-folks assumptions of postmodern belief and related techno-utopian notions each point toward what is, in effect, a disembodied future, the fact that we have different kinds of bodies might seem of diminishing significance. But this can't ultimately be our direction going forward. A key characteristic of Cultural Maturity's changes, one we will more closely examine shortly, is that they help us get more in touch with the body as experience.

We gain further insight by turning to the question of relative balance. While necessarily here we are dealing with generalities, it turns out that these generalities have great usefulness. We find greater individual variation once we leave behind polarized expectations, but we also recognize normative differences—I think of about a 60/40 balance relative to gender. Men on average tend to embody a bit more of the archetypally masculine, both its horizontal and vertical aspects; women tend on average to embody somewhat more of the archetypally feminine.

A simple way to see this 60/40 balance is to look at men's and women's bodies. Note that vertically men tend to carry their center of balance somewhat higher in the body, in the chest and shoulders, and women somewhat lower, in the pelvis and thighs. More horizontally, even with the same amount of exertion and conditioning, men's bodies tend to be a bit harder to the touch and women's a bit softer. A person could dismiss these observations as "just physical." But as CST makes clear, the notion that anything is just physical is more a product of our time in culture than how things actually work. Any "psychological" concept within CST's culturally mature formulations is, in the end, a mind/body concept.

Some of the writers who are most often cited by students of women's issues make reference to this kind of difference. For example, in her powerfully influential book *In a Different Voice*, psychologist Carol Gilligan, drawing on her studies of moral development in children, spoke of male experience in terms of "a self defined more through separation" and female experience in terms of "a self defined more by connection."[6] Linguist Deborah Tannen reached similar conclusions in her bestselling book *You Just Don't Understand: Women and Men in Conversation* in contrasting how women are more apt to use

---

6 Carol Gilligan, *In a Different Voice*, 1982, Harvard University Press, Cambridge, p. 35.

communication to establish social bonds and men are more apt to use communication to solve problems.[7]

This recognition of normative differences, while it requires that we think in ways that we may not be used to, can also be powerfully freeing. It simultaneously takes us beyond history's polarized expectations and unisex notions that in their own ways can be just as constraining. Suddenly our gender options become multitude. And our task in relationship to gender becomes newly clear and obvious: to simply be as authentically ourselves as we are able.

While this way of thinking about gender differences gets us beyond much that before has been controversial, it doesn't escape controversy entirely. I've noted that simply claiming that differences exist can be controversial in some circles. And implications when it comes to more specific gender-related questions can arouse intense feelings even among those who might not have any difficulty with the basic conclusion that I've proposed.

Current debates about equality in the workplace provide a good example. Equal opportunity and equal pay for equal work are unquestionably important goals. But we often hear it implied that the only possible explanation if we find gender differences in a profession is discrimination. Very often, discrimination *is* the major factor. But the recognition that we see normative differences also opens the door to other possibilities. For example, it suggests that choice too can play a role.

Some jobs are going be more appealing to those with more of the archetypally masculine in their makeup, others more attractive to those who most manifest the archetypally feminine. That will be the case for both men and women. But if the idea of a 60/40 normative balance is accurate, there are going to be normative differences too in the jobs men and women are drawn to. Fifty years from now, while differences will likely be much less extreme than what we see today, even if discrimination with regard to job opportunity is totally eliminated, in most professions discrepancies will likely remain. I suspect we will still see more men firefighters, computer engineers, and race car drivers. And nurses and teachers of young children will likely still more often be women.

---

7   Deborah Tannen, *You Just Don't Understand: Women and Men in Conversation*, 1990, Ballantine.

This kind of observation has implications beyond just job preference. It extends to how a person's balance of more archetypally masculine and archetypally feminine characteristics may influence more general life choices. A surprising outcome we find in Nordic countries— where gender equality is highest and best supported by social policy— is provocative in this regard. We see fewer women senior business managers, not more.[8] It appears that when women are given more choices, many will find the rat race not where they want to spend their lives. Framing these results in terms of gender archetype helps get beyond thinking only in terms of men and women. It may be that when people with more of the archetypally feminine in their makeup are given more choices, they may choose a different kind of life.

I've noted that culturally mature perspective confronts ideological correctnesses of both the political left and the political right. These reflections on gender, the workplace, and more general life choices provide good example. Those on the Left are likely to bristle at any suggestion that differences are not simply a product of discrimination. Those on the Right are more likely to feel there is something sacred in traditional roles. Framing what we see in terms of gender archetype and cultural evolution offers the possibility of thinking in more nuanced ways. In Chapter Six, I will describe how the recognition that personality style differences reflect different balances and relationships of archetypal qualities further fills out this picture by helping us better think in terms of individual variation.

Big-Picture Reflections

This chapter's examination of archetypal qualities can assist us in additional ways beyond just helping us better address gender and gender differences. It points toward important more general recognitions key to the needed "new common sense."

A first recognition should now be obvious. Each of the archetypal tendencies I've described represents a particular kind of power. In modern times, we've tended to associate power almost exclusively with the

---

8   The percentage of women senior business managers in Nordic countries is 31% compared to 43% in the United States, for example. See Nima Sananji, *The Nordic Gender Equality Paradox*, 2016, Timbro, Stockholm.

archetypally masculine. It is essential that we appreciate how the archetypally feminine is not just power, but a critical kind of power.

A second recognition addresses a key question implied by the first: Which kind of power is most important? It turns out that the answer depends on where and when we look. Where the greatest influence lies depends on the context. For example, the archetypally masculine tends to have greater influence with more in-the-world concerns such as in the traditional workplace (this for both men and women). The archetypally feminine tends to have greater influence in the home and with family (irrespective of who "wears the pants.") In relationships, it may appear that the masculine has the greater say (as with the assumption that the man will initiate), but in most instances, in fact, here too the feminine prevails (relationship is most about connectedness and few question that it is the woman who most often has the last say as far as whether a relationship will progress). Later we will see how the kind of power that has the greatest influence is also going to be different depending on the stage in the evolution of culture and on an individual's personality style.

A third recognition is needed if we are to fully appreciate the implications of the first two. Any kind of power can be used for harm as well as benefit. Obviously, the archetypally masculine can penetrate in ways that violate. But the archetypally feminine can manifest in ways that are ultimately just as destructive. It is an important topic, and we will come back to it. In Chapter Four, I will introduce the concepts of archetypally masculine and archetypally feminine violence. In Chapter Five, I will draw on the recognition that masculine and feminine power each have more vertical and horizontal aspects to tease apart multiple ways such harm can take place. And in Chapter Six, I will refine these observations further by tying them to personality style differences.

Over the course of the book, I will draw on the concept of gender archetype for an array of further observations that bring important detail to this inquiry. We will look at how the fact that each major chapter in culture's story manifests archetypally masculine and archetypally feminine qualities in different ways helps us makes sense not just of how we have thought about gender, but also how we have thought about most every aspect of our lives. We will address how appreciating this kind of big-picture pattern, along with helping us make sense of how culture has evolved, also helps us better understand what most fundamentally makes us who we are. And we will more closely examine how the kind of reflection this chapter has been about becomes possible only with Cultural Maturity's cognitive changes—and how realizing those changes represents the overarching task of our time.

CHAPTER THREE

A "Toolbox" of Needed New Skills and Capacities

A rewarding sense of identity or fulfillment in love today requires skills and capacities new to us as a species. This is a radical claim, but it follows from a related observation implied in previous chapters: Whole-Person identity and Whole-Person love both involve more than just thinking and acting differently. They require that we "hold reality" in fundamentally new, more complete—more whole-box-of-crayons—ways.

Making sense of needed new skills and capacities is critically important. Such abilities are what will let us make our way as the culturally defined guideposts of times past lose their former reliability. And the fact that these are abilities that we can practice means that just spending time with them can help us begin to engage our time's necessary next chapter in identity and love. Needed new skills and capacities also provide essential insight into the foundational nature of the changes our times are about. They help us more deeply understand what defines Cultural Maturity's changes and how the result differs from what we have known.

With this chapter, I will first describe a way in which holding reality in the more complete way that makes these skills and capacities possible can be directly facilitated. We will then turn to some of the most important of those needed new skills and capacities.

Parts Work

How do we best support Whole-Person identity and relationship? Practicing any of the new skills and capacities I will touch on gets us a long way. But it is also possible to draw on methods specifically designed to produce this result.

One of the most powerful I call simply "Parts Work." When Parts Work is done well and a person is up to the challenge, it offers almost no option but to step into Cultural Maturity's more sophisticated territory of understanding and experience—including Whole-Person identity and relationship.

Parts Work also helps us more conceptually. I've promised to more clearly define Whole-Person identity and relationship, to be more precise than just saying that each involves more consciously engaging all the crayons in our metaphorical box. Parts Work does just this. And it does so in a manner that addresses culturally mature perspective's requirement that we think in deeper and more complete ways. The kind of "definition" that Parts Work provides goes beyond just rational description to draw on the whole of our cognitive complexity.

Any thorough description of Parts Work would require a book of its own, but a glimpse helps us more deeply grasp the implications of the needed more specific new skills and capacities.[1] A simple way to think about Parts Work is that it engages the various aspects of our psyches—the crayons in the systemic box—like characters in a play.

In doing Parts Work, the person first sits in what will eventually be his or her Whole-Person (culturally mature perspective) chair. He or she is then guided in placing various parts—a curious part, an angry part, a reasonable part, a scientific part, a spiritual part—around the room. Each part is given its own chair. Through conversations with the parts, the person is facilitated in learning to consciously hold and apply his or her larger—whole-box-of-crayons—complexity.

Parts Work helps a person learn to draw deeply on the diverse sensibilities and inclinations that make that person who they are. As important, it challenges a person to recognize that in each case the viewpoints that parts represent are partial. (At a personal level, they reflect limited life perspectives. At a more cultural level, they give us ideological beliefs.[2]) Ultimately, Parts Work is about taking

---

1   *Cultural Maturity: A Guidebook for the Future* provides a more detailed introduction to Parts Work. And my upcoming volume *Creative Systems Theory: A Comprehensive Theory of Purpose, Change, and Interrelationship in Human Systems* will address the topic in depth.

2   CST defines ideology as any way of thinking that takes one part of a larger

full ownership of that Whole-Person chair and through doing this learning to live from the new, more dynamic and encompassing reality it represents.

Two cardinal rules guide the work. First, only the Whole-Person chair talks to the world. (Parts don't talk to the world, as is commonly the case with reactive responses and discourse that stops short of being culturally mature). Second, parts don't talk with other parts, only to the Whole-Person chair (think of a wagon wheel with the parts being various spokes). In doing Parts Work, the Whole-Person chair defines identity and always has the last word.

Here are a couple of brief Parts Work examples pertinent to this book's reflections, taken from work with clients:

Example #1: Mark was in his early thirties when he first came to me for therapy. Relationships thus far in his life had rarely gone well. While they might be quite close initially, after a month or so they would fall apart. He had yet to have a successful love relationship of any length. As he sat before me, he seemed unsure of himself, and also oddly distant.

After a few sessions to get acquainted, I introduced the concept of Parts Work. The first part Mark identified was a gruff old man. The old man wasn't very open to talking—other than commenting that he really didn't like women that much (or the idea of therapy).

Mark then identified a second part that had very different sentiments. It was not just attracted to women, it idealized them. It was quite romantic, indeed to an extreme. Mark was more fond of this part and commented that it was probably this part that had gotten him to come to see me.

After we had worked together over several weeks, a pattern became apparent. When Mark was initially attracted to a woman, the romantic part took charge. In effect, it was this part that was having the relationship. But within a short while the gruff old man would intercede. When he did, the relationship would become increasingly conflicted. Pretty quickly it would come to an end. When the old man was in charge, Mark was clearly not a very pleasant person to be around.

---

systemic reality and treats it as the whole of truth. See *Hope and the Future: Confronting Today's Crisis of Purpose*.

To get more deeply at what was going on, I suggested that Mark talk with the old man. Mark turned to him and asked pointedly: "What is your problem?" Mark then went over to the old man's chair to hear what he had to say.

The old man's response was simple and immediate: "When you let the romantic part take over, you do stupid things. I'm trying to keep you safe." It turned out that the old man was interfering for what was ultimately a good reason. He was protecting Mark from losing himself in what was an ultimately limited kind of connection.

Mark and I talked at length about what it might mean to relate with a woman from his Whole-Person chair rather than from just the romantic part. At first the idea confused him. It also seemed less interesting to him than what he had known. He couldn't see why this might be anything he would want. But he agreed to give it a try.

Over the ensuing weeks, Mark did further Parts Work to practice communicating from a more Whole-Person place. And he saw results. He found himself more willing to reach out to women and in general to relate to women in more caring ways. With time, he got the tangible reward of a new relationship that began to grow and endure in ways that relationships had not before.

Later Mark again talked to the gruff old man. Mark wanted to know what the old man thought about the new relationship. To his surprise, the old man had no objection. Indeed, he now liked that a woman was part of Mark's life. Even more surprising, the old man no longer seemed so gruff, or so old.

As Mark and the old man talked further, the old man shared that in truth he had liked women all along. His problem was only with how Mark didn't seem to know how to have a relationship without sacrificing his own identity to get there. He proposed to Mark that if Mark could love from his Whole-Person chair, he would not only be supportive of Mark having love in his life, he would be happy to help out in any way he could.

Example #2: Rebecca was in her mid-forties when she came to see me. She described a pattern of abusive relationships—often physically abusive—with conflict a consistent ingredient. She also described sticking with these relationships—including two marriages—in spite of the abuse.

In doing Parts Work, the first part Rebecca identified was quiet and unassuming. When Rebecca spoke to the part, it seemed passive, even submissive, in its responses. But as Rebecca continued talking with the part and reflected on times when its influence was strongest, it became clear that things were not so simple. While the part spoke as if it were a fragile victim to its circumstances, Rebecca noted a surprising result when that part took over. Somehow Rebecca felt, if not more powerful, at least more in control.

These feelings began to make sense when Rebecca talked about how relationships for her had tended to progress. Early on in a relationship, the part would act helpless in ways that certain men would find attractive. These were not men that would be ultimately healthy for Rebecca, but Rebecca saw that this was a kind of attraction that she could count on.

As Rebecca became more acquainted with this part, she found herself better understanding her role in the conflict that had so often been a part of her relationships. She saw that once a relationship began to be established, this part would often act in ways that undermined. Doing so would bring out the worst in the already not great men she had chosen to be with.

With refection, Rebecca saw, to her surprise, that there were ways in which the conflict that resulted had often served her. Certainly it helped keep her safe, guaranteed that the man would not get too close. It also brought reliable excitement. And it protected Rebecca from feeling alone. We talked about how two people who are fighting never stop thinking about each other.

With these observations, Rebecca began to have more insight into why past relationships had taken the forms that they had. She also better understood why she before had stayed in relationships even when she knew they were not healthy.[3]

---

3   This particular kind of parts-to-parts dynamic is more common than people like to admit. Think of the popularity of E.L. James' bestseller *Fifty Shades of Grey*. Such patterns can reflect normal variation in sexual preferences or, as here, protective mechanisms that get in the way of the possibility of deep connecting.

Over time in our work together, Rebecca became acquainted with other parts of herself—a creative part, a more assertive part that encouraged her to better stand up for herself, a more intellectual part that expressed frustration that Rebecca was not doing more with her life. Rebecca began to explore what it would mean to more solidly live from her own chair. She practiced making boundaries to the part that had so often before taken over. She also began to draw more consciously on all her parts in making life choices.

Rebecca saw that when she did, life was not quite so predictable. But she also saw that she was coming to like herself much better.

As far as men, Rebecca came to recognize that having a man always there for her had stopped being important in the same way. She also found herself attracted to men who in their own ways were more complete. Every now and then she missed the always predictable excitements she had known in the past. But such feelings quickly passed as she recognized what more she had become.[4]

Using Parts Work to Redefine Identity and Love

I've proposed that Parts Work, besides helping us learn to hold reality in the needed more complete way, also provides quite precise definitions for Whole-Person identity and relationship. This is definition of a functional sort rather than definition as rational description. But definition in this sense is what provides the needed precision in a culturally mature reality. Parts Work offers a concrete way to understand what needed changes involve and, in the process, clarifies just what makes Whole-Person identity and love different from what we have known.

Let's start with identity. I've proposed that changes happening today in how we think about identity are as profound in their significance as

---

4 In Chapter Six, I will describe how related kinds of change can be seen with the mature stages in any particular relationship and in a more encompassing sense with maturity in our individual development. To keep these examples brief, the work I've described does not fully support that culturally mature Whole-Person identity and love was the result. But in each case, work continued over time and with sufficient depth that what we saw was Whole-Person identity and relationship in the sense that this book is about.

those that gave us the modern concept of the individual. With them, we turn first pages in a fundamentally new chapter in how we think about who we are— and ultimately in what it means to be a person.

Parts Work provides a simple way to describe what becomes different with identity in this new sense. Our ideas about what it means to be a "self" in times past have been based on identification with parts and relationships between parts—for instance, a strong part as opposed to a weak part. In contrast, Whole-Person identity draws explicitly on a more conscious and encompassing experience of self, one based on holding and taking responsibility in the whole of one's multifaceted complexity.[5]

The defining change with Whole-Person relationship is analogous. In two-halves-make-a-whole love, some archetypal quality in one person relates to a complementary archetypal quality in the other. Most often in heterosexual relationships this would be a more archetypally masculine part in the man and a more archetypally feminine part in a woman, but it can also be the reverse.[6] Whole-Person love is about

---

5 Earlier I observed that the phrase "Whole-Person" can be confused with similar language used in psychological formulations of a more humanistic or spiritual sort. Parts Work helps make the distinction. Humanistic views tend to identify with parts that side with feelings (or with ideas that lean toward the feeling side of a feelings-versus-thoughts internal parts-to-parts conversation). Spiritual views have their roots in parts that identity with spiritual oneness. In different ways, each confuses a part that sees the world in terms of connectedness with the needed more encompassing and complete kind of wholeness that is our concern here. CST describes how polarity at its most fundamental juxtaposes difference and connectedness. Thus, in contrast to what people who identify with connectedness like to believe, identifying with connectedness quite specifically involves taking sides. It takes us no closer to mature systemic perspective than its opposite.

6 Actually, it tends to be more complex than this. I've spoken of how two-halves-make-a-whole relationship is based on projection. What we are relating to is as much a projected and idealized part in ourselves as an aspect of the other person. In addition, traditional romantic bonds tend to be "cross-polar." Commonly we see two almost opposite kinds of projection. We idealize the other—put them on a pedestal. And at once we relate to the other person as if they were a child. We see the latter in the use of diminutives such as "baby" or "dear" for our romantic partners.

relating and living from the whole of who we are, in ways that consciously draw on the whole of our complex natures.

We don't need formally facilitated Parts Work to benefit from its lessons. For example, we can practice something similar by ourselves. When I'm driving, I sometimes imagine parts sitting in various places in the car. The fact that I am holding the steering wheel substitutes for the Whole-Person chair. It helps me stay in touch with who needs to be in charge as I imagine what various parts might want to say to me and how each might contribute.

We can also apply approaches that draw informally on insights from Parts Work. For example, a high school teacher could use parts language in the classroom to engage high school students about the challenges that dating can present. The teacher might say something like this:

"I'll bet many of you have a part that finds the idea of being close with another person pretty exciting and might be tempted to do almost anything to get it to happen. And I'll bet most of you also have a part that is afraid of reaching out, afraid that you will do something that the other person might not like, or that you might be rejected and harmed in the process.

"Notice that if either kind of part gets to run the show, the result is going to be problems. If the first part calls the shots, you could miss the communication needed if you are going to be a caring and respectful person and act in ways that violate. Our you could end up with someone who is really not good for you or choose to engage in levels of closeness you are not yet ready for. If the second part calls the shots, there is a good chance you will choose to push the other person away even if in fact you would like to get to know them. And if you do choose to get close and all does not go well, you may end up blaming the other person for a situation that you may in fact be just as responsible for.

"To engage possible relationship with courage and respect, you have to recognize both of these very different kinds of parts. And there is more, the learning that is ultimately of greatest importance. You need to be ready to make your choices from a larger place that is better able to appreciate what is ultimately best for you."

The imagery of Parts Work can also be used to help us rethink beliefs of most any sort that stop short of today's needed new systemic sophistication. I've noted that the cognitive changes that produce culturally mature understanding help us get our minds around any kind of question that we've before framed in the language of polarity. Parts Work can be applied to polarities of any sort—political left versus political right, thoughts versus feelings, science versus religion. In each case, the two sides of the pertinent polarity are best thought of as parts. The more systemic picture that the Whole-Person/Whole-System chair provides makes clear that answers that come from any polarized position are inherently insufficient. It also alerts us to how, when we identify with polarized positions (or simply replace them with compromise), the ultimately important question has yet to be asked.[7]

New Skills and Capacities

Let's turn now to specific needed new skills and capacities. I'll start with new skills and capacities necessary for the day-to-day tasks of Whole-Person identity and love and then briefly address a few that relate more specifically to the forms and structures of a culturally mature life. The significance of each of those I will describe follows directly from how reality changes with culturally mature perspective—put in Parts Work terms, when we are able to sit in Parts Work's Whole-Person chair. Importantly for the possibility of success with the tasks ahead, so does making each of them manifest in our lives.

Skill #1: Learning to Draw on More Complete Kinds of Truth

Success with each of these new skills and capacities in the end depends on how effectively we engage the first. We can put it in terms of a question: On just what do we base our choices when one-size-fits-all cultural rules and two-halves-make-a-whole projections no longer serve us? We can ask the same question from the perspective of Parts Work. We want to know what remains to guide us when we step beyond the ready answers of parts and engage life from that Whole-Person chair.

I used the perhaps overly philosophical-seeming word "truth" in naming this skill because truth is ultimately what we are talking about. But this is necessary truth in Cultural Maturity's more systemic sense.

---

7 See *Hope and the Future: Confronting Today's Crisis of Purpose* or *Cultural Maturity: A Guidebook for the Future* for a more detailed look at these results and their implications.

We could substitute the word "measure." CST uses the more general term "referent" and speaks of the need for newly "integrative referents."

Needed new truths are different in fundamental ways. Most obviously, they are more encompassing. They require that we better take into account the whole of who we are and also the whole of whatever we wish to consider. As important, they necessarily involve new levels of responsibility. We've always been responsible for our choices, but in times past, culture as parent has made the larger portion of them for us. With Whole-Person love and identity, we become responsible not just for making good choices, but for determining what for us makes a choice good. In addition, these new truths require that we be much more comfortable with the fact of uncertainty. They necessarily leave behind the one-size-fits-all order and predictability that clear guideposts have traditionally provided.

Engaging truth in this more mature and complete sense highlights an apparent paradox that I noted in the first chapter. Needed new truths are at once more complex and simpler than what they replace. When we step into culturally mature territory, the measures on which we base our choices become more multifaceted. And at the same time, they are more direct, more bare-boned.

We find this with both identity and love. The choices of identity involve greater complexity because we recognize more possibilities. They also draw more consciously on our own complexity, the multiplicity of parts that make up who we are—all the crayons in our particular systemic box. But at the same time, identity's choices become more straightforward. When we better engage all that is involved, truth becomes what fits, what works. The actions and choices that are most supportive and affirming of our particular life become truth's bottom line.

It is similar with love. As far as complexity, not only do past rules fail us, the whole romantic ideal that before has given us our basis for choosing fails us. Suddenly, we must take much more into account, both in the world and in ourselves. But when we do, our choices again in important ways become more straightforward. With Whole-Person love, ultimately what we want to measure is simply what we share, the degree to which a connection is creative and vital. We feel love when a relationship in some way creates new life, when one plus one becomes more than two.

We can draw on a formal philosophical notion to describe truth in this new sense, but for the notion to work we have to radically redefine it. The Whole-Person chair in Parts Work engages us in what is ultimately a "pragmatic" enterprise. With both Whole-Person identity and Whole-Person love, truth becomes a simple reflection of what works. The difference from how the word "pragmatic" is conventionally used is that this is not simply a logical or expedient kind of pragmatism, but rather a "life-centered" pragmatism. The Whole-Person chair's job is to discern the choices that are most life-affirming and to act on this most essential kind of information.[8]

Skill #2: Learning to Engage Identity and Love as Exploratory Processes

Whole-Person identity and love each require being more comfortable with change. Culturally mature perspective makes us more conscious of how identity and love are never ultmately fixed—they are processes. It also helps us appreciate how identity and love are in the end specifically "creative" kinds of processes. For them to work most powerfully, we must engage them as exploration.

With identity, the fact that culture's answers can't be enough means that any clear sense of self must involve learning and questioning. And figuring out what matters is necessarily a life-long process, not a one-time thing. We recognize a more limited version of this greater humility to change's role in identity in the wisdom that can accompany personal maturity. With Cultural Maturity, we confront its importance in a more fully encompassing sense.

Whole-Person love requires greater comfort with change most obviously in how it makes changes ongoing role inescapable. This quote from Anne Morrow Lindbergh hangs outside my office door to help remind people that change in love is real, and also ultimately not to be feared:

"When you love someone, you do not love them all the time in exactly the same way.... It is an impossibility. It is even a lie to pretend to. And yet this is exactly what most of us demand. We have so little

---

8 *Cultural Maturity: A Guidebook for the Future* examines this essential distinction in depth and provides further examples.

faith in the ebb and flow of life, of love, of relationships. We leap at the flow of the tide and resist in terror at its ebb. We are afraid it will never return. We insist on permanency, or duration, or continuity, when the only continuity possible, in life as in love, is in growth, in fluidity—in freedom in the sense that dancers are free, often hardly touching when they pass yet partners ultimately in the same patterns."[9]

A more exploratory picture confronts us too with how we need to be sensitive to just what love at different points requires of us. For example, with love's beginnings, we've tended to idealize love at first sight. But while initial attraction can be nice, knowing another person for who they are rather than as a projected ideal can take time. When I look back over love relationships in my life, I see that most often I didn't know the other person with any depth until many months together, and frequently years. And, even then, there could be major surprises.

When a young person I am working with in therapy frets about whether someone they have just met is right for them, I often offer that they are asking the wrong question, or at least one that is premature. I also suggest that the right question is simpler. All they really need to know is whether they want to get together with the person again. If the young person is doing Parts Work, a quick conversation with the parts usually provides an answer to this more time-appropriate—and more exploratory—question.

In Chapter Six, I will briefly describe how we can think about love as a creative process more explicitly in the sense that it tends to go through predictable stages. We don't need that level of discernment to be successful in love, but it helps if we can at least be more accepting of the fact that "love has its seasons."

The recognition that love is best thought of as an exploratory process raises important further questions. We can wonder, for example, just what in times ahead will serve as the glue in the bonds of intimacy, the basis for love. I've described how two-halves-make-a-whole dynamics have offered not just that we fit together like two matching puzzle pieces, but that a predictable kind of magnetism will hold those pieces together. With Whole-Person love's more exploratory picture, we lose such easy predictability.

---

9 Anne Morrow Lindbergh, *Gift from the Sea*, New York: Pantheon, 1991, First edition 1955.

Could it be that just as we are coming to the place of greatest potential for fully personal intimate love, we are losing any reason to take the risks? Clearly there is still sex. But for the task of really deep bonding, our erotic touchings are rarely enough.

The answer to how love in a more exploratory world could have a chance must lie with ways love's new picture adds to what we have known. I've described how love that manifests from Whole-Person identity—love that is based on loving another person directly for who they are rather than as idealized possibility—is potentially much deeper. In this sense, love expressed from that Whole-Person chair is also more ultimately romantic. In addition, the fact that Whole-Person love is more consciously pragmatic, more attentive to actual needs that love fulfills (companionship, intimate bonds, parental cooperation, and so on) means that it can be much more resilient. Add to these factors how stepping beyond the one-size-fits-all cultural dictates of times past invites a greater variety of options in how we approach love and we find legitimate reason to be optimistic.

A related question concerns commitment. It is reasonable to ask what commitment looks like in a reality where change is such a constant presence. On first encountering the concept of Whole-Person relationship, people can express concern that the idea seems to leave out commitment. Ultimately, as we shall see, it does almost the opposite. Yet the question of just what commitment becomes with Whole-Person relationship is a good one.

Later we will examine how there can be many specific kinds of commitments, some more traditional, others less so, depending on the people and their particular circumstances. But Parts Work also brings attention to a more basic kind of commitment. With Whole-Person relationship, we commit to loving from that Whole-Person chair. We promise to do our best to engage the other person from the whole of who we are and also to do all we can to protect the other person from incursion by our parts. Such commitment requires that we hold experience more complexly than has before been necessary. But again, it is also about keeping things simple—in the best sense.

A more exploratory relationship to identity and love makes considerable demands. Fortunately, Cultural Maturity's changes also make those demands more tolerable. Indeed, it can make them fascinating. And the rewards for taking on these demands are great—identity and love that are more complete, more vital, and ultimately more fun.

Skill #3: Getting Better at Knowing and Expressing
Our "Yeses" and "Nos"

Nothing more defines culturally mature decision-making than the need to be more conscious and explicit in our discernments. Put simply, we need to do a better job of recognizing and articulating our yeses and nos. This is the case equally with identity and love.

Engaging identity as an exploratory process is in the end about nothing more than making ongoing yes and no choices. We venture forth and each step along the way note what works for us and what does not. Put in Parts Work terms, the Whole-Person chair is engaged in a constant process of discerning what choices are most life-affirming, and accepting or rejecting options accordingly.

It is similar with relationship. If you ask people what ability is most important to good relationship, most will answer something like "clear communication." But we can be more specific, and we need to be if our concern is relationship in today's new relationship landscape. Success at love more and more requires being skilled at discerning and articulating our yeses and nos.

In times past, traditional roles and relationship assumptions have delineated the most important yeses and nos for us. Today, as traditional guideposts abandon us, relationship's yeses and nos increasingly become our responsibility not just to determine, but also to voice. Fail to do so and we quickly get ourselves into trouble. Clarity with regard to yeses and nos becomes particularly important if our interest is Whole-Person relationship.[10]

This needed new clarity brings with it an important implication that we can easily miss. It requires both men and women to give up traditional kinds of power. This is most obvious for traditional male power. For

___

10 Later we will look more closely at some of the various forms violence of both the archetypally masculine and archetypally feminine sorts can take. It turns out that the explicit articulation of yeses and nos provides an effective antidote for the great majority of different ways we can do harm to one another.

example, if a man takes on the traditional task of initiating, he has to be keenly aware of and deeply respectful of the woman's nos. That means sincerely wanting to hear "no" if that is the woman's honest response, and honoring it. In the old, more heroic picture, his task might be more to see if he could find a way around or through the woman's defenses. In the new picture, not only are nos respected, the man makes every effort to be sure he is getting clear yeses every step along the way.

But men are not alone in this need to rethink power. Indeed, in an important sense, today's needed new clarity requires of women an even greater giving up of traditional power. We've seen how the fact that archetypally feminine power tends to be less explicit is key to its great ability to affect. Women (and men who make use of archetypally feminine power) are taught not to reveal their intentions, something I've observed with the common guidance given to women that they should "play hard to get." I reflected in an earlier footnote on how I often work with young men who find themselves totally bewildered by today's changing rules and expectations. The fact that the information they need is so often kept out of sight can make their task almost impossible. Clear yeses and nos mean the woman, like the man, must be willing to lay her cards on the table. She doesn't get to have it both ways if she wants her nos to be respected.[11]

I've promised to elaborate on some of the complexities that must be included in our considerations if today's conversations about gender and sexuality are to have the needed sophistication. These reflections on the need to be more conscious and explicit with our yeses and nos highlight a couple of these complexities.

The first is simply how rapidly assumptions and expectations are changing.

I recently passed a young woman on the street wearing a tee shirt that proclaimed "There is no fine line." It would be wonderful if this were so, if there were a clear set of rules that everyone agrees on. But, in fact, our yes and no assumptions are in rapid flux. And even with the more delineated rules of times past, there was much less agreement

---

11 With each of these assertions, we can just as appropriately replace my references to men and women with other gender identifications or sexual orientations.

than we tend to imagine. In our conversations about gender and love, we must be humble to how easy it can be to miscommunicate even with the best of intentions.

The second added complexity relates to the less explicit ways in which archetypally feminine power has often been expressed. Not only can we miscommunicate because expectations are changing, we can miscommunicate because in the old reality, communicating clearly— indeed, often just knowing consciously what one wanted and might want to communicate—was not how things were done. In this context, the needed clarity as far as both yeses and nos becomes an even greater challenge. We can easily miss this further complexity because of how distanced we are from the archetypally feminine in our time.

I should be clear about something I am not implying with this emphasis on good communication and sensitivity to yeses and nos. Today, we can hear proposals that come frighteningly close to advocating legal contracts for each step toward possible intimacy. This is not what I am suggesting. I can't imagine anything more deadening to intimacy as exploration. What I *am* suggesting is that communication in relationship needs to be much more conscious and nuanced—more personal, more deeply engaged, and more demanding of responsibility—than we've assumed before. An ethic that unquestioningly respects nos combined with a commitment on everyone's part to make yeses and nos explicit should with time get us where we need to go.

Skill #4: Avoiding Overwhelm

A further needed new skill relates to a kind of discernment that takes on new levels of importance with Cultural Maturity's changes. We need a keen sensitivity to the resources that at any moment we have available to us. A formal CST notion—what it calls Capacitance—lets us be more precise. Capacitance describes the amount of life we can take in before things become too much. Think of a balloon, that if blown up too big, threatens to pop.

Attention to Capacitance becomes newly important with Whole-Person identity and relationship. While it is never a healthy thing to be stressed beyond what one can handle, being overwhelmed makes staying in one's Whole-Person chair almost impossible. Parts will step in to protect us. The flip side of parts limiting us when they take over is that their taking over provides protection from realities that are too big for us to tolerate. If Whole-Person identity and relationship is important to us, living our lives in a way that honors Capacitance becomes essential.

The topic of Capacitance is often a focus when I work with people wishing to develop culturally mature abilities—how to discern it, how to manage it, and how, when we lack needed Capacitance, we can avoid doing harm to ourselves or others. We can think of attention to Capacitance as another essential aspect of commitment in culturally mature relationship (certainly in relationships with others, but also with oneself).

I'll share a Capacitance-related story that graphically brings together the themes covered thus far in this chapter, most obviously the importance of clear yeses and nos, but even more, and in a particularly striking way, what can happen when systems are overwhelmed and parts intercede. It also highlights a further kind of complexity that we need to acknowledge if today's conversations about gender and sexuality are to have the needed sophistication.

The story comes from early in my twenties and involves a particularly confusing and unsettling sexual/relationship encounter. I'd gone out with a young woman of about my age for around a month when she invited me back to her apartment. She initiated hugging on the couch and then invited me back into her bedroom, She suggested we take off our clothes and we slid into bed together.

I was struck with how easily the sexual connection progressed given that it was our first time together. Her body was highly responsive to my touch and the broad smile on her face and the sounds she made as we moved together made it pretty clear that she was enjoying the connection as much as I. We made love several times, enthusiastically and often wildly.

As we lay there afterward, I asked her how she was doing, expecting something on the order of "wow, that was amazing." Instead she sat up and said, "I think you raped me."

I could not have been more startled at her response and hardly knew what to say. I remember fumbling for words and being able only to come up with something defensive like—"What? It was your idea and you could have said no at any point. And you certainly looked like you were enjoying yourself." After a long, awkward silence, I just got up and left.

If nothing else, this story highlights how complex and problematical circumstances can become even without any obvious ill intent. When I now look back, I think I better understand what happened. She was not terribly experienced with relationship, and I suspect the intensity of the physical connection overwhelmed her. I also suspect that she was in a part when she so enthusiastically got things started (as we tend to be, particularly at that age). When things got to be too much, another much less friendly part took over to protect her.

I felt sad about the experience afterward. She had seemed a good person and in spite of the unfortunate direction things had gone, I never felt that she had been consciously manipulative or had intended to deceive. I suspect that if we had been a bit older, things might have progressed quite differently. There is a good chance we could have better communicated, weathered the circumstances, and even continued to be friends. Put in the context of this chapter, imagine how differently things might have gone if Whole-Person perspective had prevailed, parts had not interceded, and needed yeses and nos, whatever they might have been, had been better recognized and clearly articulated.

I noted that this example illustrates another of the complexities that we need to include in today's conversations about gender and sexuality. In the great majority of instances when someone experiences violation, they are to be taken at their word and believed. But it is also the case that in many different ways, psychological dynamics can interfere with our ability to see clearly.

Skill #5: Learning to Manage Asymmetries

I include the next new skill less because of its specific significance than because it helps with further understanding what Whole-Person relationship requires of us. It is perhaps again best put as a question: How does Whole-Person relationship change when one person is fairly adept with Whole-Person relating and the other person is less so?

The answer might seem surprising. In fact, very little changes. It turns out that Whole-Person relationship does not ultimately require two people. Mutuality is wonderful, and with it much more becomes possible. But this can't always be the case. Any time we engage another person from Parts Work's Whole-Person chair, we can usefully think of the result as at least a form of Whole-Person relating.

The implications of this observation are going to be different depending on the kind of relationship. For example, when a relationship is between a parent and a child, significant Capacitance difference is what we expect. And significant discrepancies in Capacitance—and more specifically, differences in people's capacity for Whole-Person relationship—need not be a great problem when relating with neighbors or someone we encounter at the grocery store.

With a life partner, the challenges presented by significant Capacitance differences are going to be of greater consequence. They may even point toward a relationship being ultimately unworkable. Certainly they call for particular care if the connection is to work. But the basic notion that nothing really changes still holds. This observation acquires added relevance with the recognition that at different times we are all going to be more or less capable of Whole-Person relating. In the end, being overly concerned with whether our partner is always in their Whole-Person chair is good evidence that we are not really in ours.

Skill (set) #6: More Structural Skills and Capacities

Most of the new skills and capacities I have described are most pertinent to how we go about making everyday choices. But some of the most important new skills and capacities relate more to the choices through which we give our lives structure. In times past, we rarely questioned life structures fundamentally. Culture told us what jobs were to be preferred, the kind of house it was ideal to live in, and what love should look like, whether when dating or in marriage, Today, as cultural dictates becomes less explicit and options multiply, we need to choose more consciously if the structures of our lives are to work.

Here I will focus primarily on the structures of relationship, though because relationship structures so often determine broader life choices, in the end they are just as much about identity. When I work with individuals and couples around relationship issues, I give particular attention to three structure-related concerns. For ease of conversation, I will call them simply the "rhythm, boundary, and container" aspects of relationship. They are significant because they address structures systemically, not just in terms of possible forms, but in terms of underlying organizational principles. They overlap, but each provides a somewhat different vantage for getting beyond traditional expectations and crafting life structures appropriate to the lives of particular people. We can think of the ability to consciously ask questions of the rhythm, boundary, and container sort as another needed new capacity.[12]

• *Rhythms*

When I work with a couple, one of the things I often first ask about is the rhythms of their relationship—how much time they spend together and spend apart. In my experience, when two people get the rhythms of relationship just right—when they spend just the right amount of time together, and when they are together, do the things that most matter to them—everything else tends to take care of itself.

Needed adjustments can be very different depending on the people and their life circumstances. For example, if a couple works and has children, the time they spend together can frequently be much less than they might imagine. Just noting this fact can take things a long way. The solution to relationship issues in these situations may be no more complicated than each person making the other more of a priority.

In other instances, just the opposite can be the case. The issue may be too much time together rather than too little. This is often the situation when there is significant conflict in relationship. Conflict may be serving to provide needed separation. At least getting started with a solution can be just as simple: more time for separate activities—a regular night out with friends, now and then a trip alone, whatever works.

One of the best indicators of a healthy relationship—and the possibility of successful Whole-Person relationship—is just how fully rhythmic the relationship can be. Closeness and separateness each in their own ways require Capacitance and create vulnerability. Low-Capacitance relationships tend to keep things at a safe middle distance. They don't let things get too close, and neither do they allow for fully separate identities. High-Capacitance relationships can transition from being very close to being wholly separate to again being close without major catches in the process.

---

12 I examine "rhythm, boundary, and container" questions more deeply in *Cultural Maturity: A Guidebook for the Future.*

• *Boundaries*

Another thing I often ask about earlier on as a therapist is how comfortable people are with boundaries. I addressed more everyday boundaries with our look at the importance of clearly articulating yeses and nos. But being conscious in making boundaries of a more structural sort is just as important. As with rhythms, it is surprising how often when people get boundaries right, everything else takes care of itself.

The recognition that it is important for your partner to have his or her private thoughts—and you to have yours—can be thought of as a structural boundary recognition. And structural boundaries can also be more concrete. Having a "room of one's own" in which to be creative, keep one's special things, and live with those private thoughts has saved many a marriage. Whole-Person relationship requires greater sensitivity to the importance of structural boundaries—both establishing good ones and honoring the structural boundaries of others.

The importance of boundaries can be difficult to grasp for some people. We can think of boundaries as some opposite of freedom. And we tend to identify intimacy with the dissolving of boundaries. But, in fact, real freedom requires good boundaries, and intimacy is not possible without them. The image of a cell's outer membrane helps capture the essential relationship between yeses and nos of a more structural sort. The cell must be able to let things in for it to be vital. But these must be the right things at the right times if the cell is to maintain its integrity. Real yeses become possible only if a person is comfortable with and effective in establishing needed nos.

• *Containers*

Container questions are the most explicitly structural. Marriage provides one common answer to this kind of question, as do familiar categories we use in the process of getting to know someone, such as "dating" or "just being friends." But as cultural assumptions become less cut and dried, these stop being the only right answers. With Cultural Maturity's changes, it becomes ever more important to be creative in how we think about our container options. Whole-Person bonds invite—indeed, demand—that people create containers that more specifically honor two unique people and their unique connection.

Recently I worked with an older woman who bemoaned how limited her options were in growing up. She had felt that she had really had two only choices. She could be married with a husband who was the provider, a house with a white picket fence, and the proverbial 2.2 children. Or she could be a "spinster." She commented how lucky women were today to have so many more possibilities. Fortunately, she was someone who was sufficiently stubborn by nature that she had always found ways to structure her life so that it worked for her in spite of how culture had defined her options.

Relationship-related container questions ask about the choices and agreements that might be most consistent with two people's needs. They concern the appropriateness of traditional marriage, whether a couple wants to have children, where people wish to live, how each person chooses to spend their time, and the physical spaces that might best support how each person lives, loves, works, and plays. With Whole-Person identity and relationship, very traditional containers may work just fine. But we also may want to try out different options. Actor Jack Nicholson once observed that he thought the best arrangement for a marriage was living just far enough apart that it took a vigorous walk to get together. It is surprising how often people I work with think that sounds like a pretty good approach.[13]

Capacities and Possibility

All these capacities are new and require levels of responsibility and sophistication that have not before been needed. But they also make much more possible. And in important ways, they can make things simpler. When we successfully take them on, very often the more everyday specifics of being together take care of themselves.

---

13 With Chapter Six's look at personality style differences, we will see why Nicholson in particular might have found this arrangement appealing.

CHAPTER FOUR

Big-Picture Perspective— Gender and the Creative Evolution of Culture

Here I endeavor to put our stories about identity, gender, and love in historical context. Stepping back in this way will help us more directly understand how our ideas about identity, gender, and love have been products of how we think—or more precisely how we have thought at different times in the past. It will also help us more deeply grasp just what has been different in the beliefs of previous times, and just what needs to be different as we look to the future.

These reflections will necessarily be a bit more conceptual than those thus far. I'll draw more directly than I have in previous chapters on Creative Systems Theory's evolutionary thinking. And this being a short book, we will necessarily proceed at a lickety-split pace. But even this decidedly abbreviated treatment will have major implications for our tasks with this book. For example, with regard to the controversial question of gender differences, it will shed important further light on how differences we see have deeper roots than just conditioning. And with regard to oppression and discrimination, it will help us better understand what we have seen through history and how we can respond in the most beneficial ways to current circumstances. In addition, it will highlight how this book's reflections on gender and love can provide important insights for understanding and addressing what our times ask of us more broadly.

After some introductory theoretical reflections, I will turn specifically to how our relationship to the masculine and the feminine has evolved over time. We'll then look briefly at a few historical patterns of a more behavioral sort—such as patterns in how sexuality is viewed—

and tie these to what I have described. Finally, I'll address what the progression we've looked at can teach us about the challenges and possibilities identity, gender, and love present going forward.

On the Evolution of Archetype

For the major portion of these historical reflections, I will again draw on gender archetype as our way in. The evolution of archetype represents a different way of looking at history than we are used to. Just how it is different makes it a particularly powerful lens for viewing the history of gender and love.

To start, the evolution of archetype provides a more encompassing kind of vantage for understanding the past. In modern times, we've tended to view history almost exclusively through an archetypally masculine lens—as a chronicling of inventions, leaders, and wars. The evolution of archetype helps us approach history in terms of more fundamental changes in how we understand ourselves, each other, and the world around us.

The evolution of archetype also helps tease apart underlying patterns. That includes patterns in what got us to where we reside today and also patterns that we see in current goings-on. The evolution of archetype helps us understand, for example, both why in times past we have viewed gender through the lens of polarized projections and why the pictures that have resulted have been different at different times. It also helps us understand how this picture continues to change in our time.

CST's developmental framework will provide the "pattern language" for these reflections. The theory is particularly appropriate for our task in that it draws on both archetypally masculine and archetypally feminine sensibilities. More specifically for our task, it describes how polarities in human systems juxtapose archetypally masculine and archetypally feminine characteristics and delineates how they do so in specific ways at different times and places. The theory also addresses how the more integrative, Whole-Person/Whole-System picture I have described is not just possible but predicted going forward. I've written in great detail about this progression through the years, starting with *The Creative Imperative*.

Before we turn to how gender archetype relates to such pattern, we should first address the more basic fact of polarity—why we see polarity in the first place and how it has served us. CST proposes that the reason we tend to think in the language of polarity follows directly from what most makes us human—our tool-making, meaning-making, we could say simply "creative," natures. It delineates how a related sequence of polar dynamics organizes experience over the course of any kind of human developmental process—from individual psychological development, to how human relationships grow over time, to the evolution of culture. It also makes the essential—and radical—observation that what we witness with each of these developmental processes parallels what we find over the course of any human formative—creative—process.

Described most briefly, any creative/formative process begins with what we already know—in an original unity. Polarity first appears with the initial budding off of new possibility. Then, as the newly created form gradually pushes away from the context from which it was born and new possibility becomes solidly established, polarity too becomes more solid and established. Eventually, the task shifts to that of finishing and detail. The newly completed object increasingly now takes center stage, and attention moves even further away from creation's original context.

Importantly, change doesn't end there. There are also further stages that we can miss if we focus only on the object being created. These stages become particularly significant if our interest lies with the specific challenges of our time. The finished form must somehow reconnect with the creative context from which it arose, both past forms from which it pushed away to become something separate and the organizational realities in ourselves from which it was born.

We have common everyday language for this important result. What before seemed wholly new and distinct becomes "second nature." CST proposes that the "growing up" on which our future depends reflects this specifically integrative kind of dynamic—the newly created thing that becomes second nature in this case being the human endeavor as a whole. In every sphere, we confront the need to hold reality in more whole-box-of-crayons ways.

The language of gender archetype lets us bring greater nuance to this progression. It also helps us recognize how this creative picture might relate to questions of identity, gender, and love. It turns out that the gender qualities I introduced in Chapter Two evolve in characteristic ways over the course of any formative process. That includes not just how the particular characteristics we see at different times evolve, but also how archetypally masculine and archetypally feminine qualities relate in predictably different ways depending on when we look. Here I'll add more specific creative language. Again, a briefest of outlines must suffice.

With what we could call creative process's "incubation stage," the archetypally feminine is the dominant presence. Any formative process begins in mystery and the unformed. With creation's "inspiration stage," the archetypally feminine remains primary, but our attention turns increasingly toward that which is being newly created. At this stage, we experience the archetypally feminine and the archetypally masculine as working in harmony to bring new possibility into first form. With the next stage, what we could call creation's "perspiration stage," the newly created form struggles into solid manifestation. Because this stage requires that the newly created thing clearly separate from its original context, the relationship between polar qualities tends here to be more conflicted—at the midpoint of this stage, archetypally feminine and archetypally masculine juxtapose as at once opposing and conspiring forces. Once form is solidly established, creation then proceeds into what we could call its "finishing and polishing" stages. Here the archetypally masculine's world of material delineation and refinement increasingly predominates. As tensions subside, the archetypally feminine can again be more acknowledged, but its role is now clearly secondary, more decorative.

We can similarly describe formative process's more integrative stages using the language of gender archetype. With the process through which the new created entity begins to become "second nature," we gradually become able to step back from both the archetypally masculine and the archetypally feminine. When we do, we better appreciate the power and importance of each of them. We are also able to recognize their ultimately complementary and co-causal—we might say "procreative"—relationship.[1]

---

1 It may not be immediately obvious why we can use the language of gender archetype in this way to address the workings of formative process. CST makes the needed connection. It describes how what gives the archetypally

This chapter's historical and theoretical observations will require some committed reflection. But drawing on the evolution of archetype in this way will make such commitment well worth the effort. With regard to this book's reflections on gender, these observations will add essential nuance. I've argued that our ideas about men and women in times past have been products more of polarized projections—projections of gender archetypes—than what being a man or a woman is actually about. Much in what we have seen in times past is an expression of the historical need for complementing roles and the particulars of culturally specific beliefs. But we also find underlying patterns as a function of how gender archetypes manifest differently at different times in culture's evolutionary story.

In the progression we will examine, three themes are directly pertinent to our historical understanding of gender and relationships between the sexes. First is how the relative balance between archetypally feminine and archetypally masculine qualities follows a predictable sequence with any formative process, with the archetypally feminine playing the larger role early on and the archetypally masculine gradually assuming the greater influence with creation's more manifest stages. Second is how the felt relationship between poles also evolves in characteristic ways with essential implications for how we experience each pole. At various times, the relationship can be close and complementary, it can involve struggle and contention, or it can seem to reflect very little relationship at all. Third is how integrative dynamics help us see a larger picture and appreciate how the relationship between the archetypally feminine and archetypally masculine through history, in spite of its often dramatic and conflicted twists and turns, has been complementary—in the end, a (creative) conspiracy.

This evolving picture will help put our understanding of gender in motion. Of particular importance as we look to the future, it will help

---

masculine and the archetypally feminine the qualities I've observed is that they reflect the two halves inherent to any creative juxtaposition—on one hand, the emerging created form, on the other, creation's generative ground. In the end, any polarity juxtaposes qualities we identity more with delineation and separation with qualities we associate more with oneness and connectedness.

put the changes I've described as reordering identity, gender, and love in our time in larger perspective. It will help us make sense of why we see the particular changes that we do. It will also support my claims that these changes are predicted and ultimately serve us.[2]

Historical Perspective

CST calls its creatively based framework for understanding change and its workings developmental/evolutionary perspective. A brief outline of what it describes over the course of culture's story follows. To have a concise and precise language for stages,[3] I will use CST's formal nomenclature: Pre-Axis (for creation's "incubation" stage), Early-Axis (for creation's "inspiration" stage), Middle-Axis (for creation's "perspiration" stage), and Late-Axis (for creation's "finishing and polishing" stage). I will focus primarily on the evolution of "vertical" polar relationships to keep things simple (though we could as easily emphasize the horizontal).[4]

Again, as with Chapter's Two's introduction to the concept of gender archetype, I will draw heavily on the language of myth and symbol. Doing so provides a way to think about culture's evolutionary picture that gives a direct voice to both archetypally masculine and archetypally feminine sensibilities.

For these descriptions to help us, it will be critical throughout that we keep the essential distinction between gender and gender archetype clearly in mind. Again, these are qualities that both men and women possess. Indeed, as I've suggested, depending on a person's personality

---

2 Earlier I noted that drawing on CST, besides helping us address gender and love, also provides important support for the easily controversial ideas of CST. This is particularly the case for the specifically developmental notions I will draw on in this chapter. If you find these notions helpful, that provides important evidence for the accuracy of the approach.

3 And also to have a language we can translate to other contexts. In Chapter Six, for example, I will draw on this same language when we examine the implications of personality style differences.

4 In Chapter Six I will touch on how we see this same creative progression underlying how any love relationship evolves and also in how love tends to be different at different stages in personal development.

style, men can manifest more of the archetypally feminine and women more of the archetypally masculine. But as long as we don't forget this essential distinction, the evolution of gender archetype provides perspective for understanding identity, gender, and love that is very hard to achieve in other ways.

Creative "Incubation" (Pre-Axis)

 As a poet, I hold the most archaic values on earth. They go back to the Paleolithic; the fertility of the soil, the magic of animals, the power-vision in solitude, the terrifying initiation and rebirth, the love and ecstasy of the dance, the common work of the tribe.

—Gary Snyder

Any formative process begins before the appearance of creation as form—in original wholeness. In a creative task, this is wholeness within the known (the new is germinating within, but has yet to fully appear). In individual development, this is wholeness with the maternal bond—in the womb and with the first months of life. Put in the language of gender archetype, creation begins in the deepest reaches of the archetypally feminine.

Pre-Axis in culture extends from our earliest Stone Age times into formal civilization's first intimations and as yet barely differentiated beginnings. During this period, the relationship to wholeness and to the archetypally feminine is total, manifesting at once as wholeness with the earth, with the tribe, and with the body. Deific symbols take the form of either images that personify human experience in the "mother" language of nature (deer, bear, or raven, the breath of the wind, the spirit of the forest), or representations of the great goddess, abundant of hip and breast.[5] The tribe more than its individual members is primary. (To be excluded from the tribe is seen as tantamount to nonexistence.) And in a very important sense, reality is bodily reality. It is not possible to be part of a tribe without knowing its songs and dances.

---

5 The most recognized being the "Venus of Willendorf" from about 30,000 BCE found in Willendorf, Germany.

This unbroken wholeness also manifests in our relationship to time. In tribal realities, each season and each generation is seen as reenacting the same timeless story. Mythologist Mircea Eliade described this primordial relationship to time in this way in The Sacred and the Profane, "In a certain sense, it is even possible to say that nothing new happens in this world ... this repetition constantly maintains the world in the same auroral instant of beginnings."[6]

Creative "Inspiration" (Early-Axis)

 The word for universe is Au-Ki. It means heaven and earth. The naming of man cannot take place until the two are separated.
                          —From a Sumerian creation myth

With Early-Axis, newly created possibility steps forth from mystery into the light. The beginnings of Early-Axis appropriately bring excitement—new form has been born. Early-Axis also brings first separation. Before, the archetypally feminine was everything—we were it and immersed in it. Now there is it and something else. Newly created form comes to sit in juxtaposition to the primordial ground of its origins. Early-Axis is the most explicitly creative of formative process's stages.

Early-Axis in the evolution of culture begins with the coming together of bands and tribes into broader alliances and the appearance of early civilizations. It reaches its full flowering with the classical high cultures of both West and East. When we imagine Early-Axis times, it is grand and inspiring structures and dramatic ritual sites that come most immediately to mind—the pyramids of Egypt and Greece's Parthenon, the dramatic monuments of pre-Columbian MesoAmerica or Angkor Wat in what is now Cambodia.

Throughout this stage, the archetypally feminine remains the stronger force, something we witness in the rich artistry and deep spirituality common to Early-Axis cultures. But we also see the beginnings of clear

---

6 Mircea Eliade, *The Sacred and the Profane: The Nature of Religion*, 1957, Harvest/HBJ Publishers.

distinction between poles. Such distinction finds initial expression in the simple fact of civilization's rise—nature and humanity for the first time become distinct. It manifests more audaciously later in this stage with the elevated splendor that so commonly marks cultural expression.

Over the course of Early-Axis, we see a gradual progression from obvious archetypally feminine preeminence to realities in which the archetypally masculine gradually plays a more explicit role. Classical Greece provides a good place to witness this progression. (I think of classical Greek civilization beginning just at the end of pre-history—Pre-Axis—and extending through Early-Axis.) Over the span of classical Greek culture, the gods became increasingly ascendant. They also more and more became human, and male.

During earliest times, the primary deity was the earth goddess Gaia. The pantheons of gods had not yet taken up residence atop Olympus. Homer speaks of Gaia as the "universal mother, firmly founded, the oldest of divinities." During the middle years of Greek flowering, the pantheon settled in its familiar lofty abode. With that ascent, male figures increasingly assumed positions of greater influence, though the realms below generally maintained female representation. Later the female mythic keepers of the underworld were replaced by male overlords—Poseidon for the sea, Hades for the earthly underworld, Dionysus for the wisdom of the body and intuition. By the later years of Greece's eminence, the transposition had become virtually complete. Zeus resided as supreme patriarch, his ascendency only slightly tempered by the persuasions of his wife Hera, the most powerful remaining female figure on Olympus.[7]

But while the archetypally masculine assumes greater influence over the course of Early-Axis in culture, it remains the case that mystery is always present and most often still prevails. For example, while at the peak of classical Greek culture male gods were ascendant, to find wis-

---

7 Upper Pole characteristics came to take especially strong expression for their time in classical Greece. Because of this, ancient Greece makes a particularly good place to recognize this emerging significance of the archetypally masculine. By the time of Plato and Aristotle, we see further evolution in this direction as more philosophical sensibilities began to eclipse the mythic.

dom a person still consulted the mysterious, female Oracle of Delphi. Indeed, because at this stage we now juxtapose the light and the dark, mystery's dark power can be felt in ways that are even more pronounced than previously. In the vertical, mystery now has a specific orientation. It is something that, when we are identifying with the conscious Upper Pole of experience, we specifically stand upon and exist in relationship to. It speaks as the underworld of existence.

We see this greater contrast between the light and the dark reflected in new ways in which the archetypally feminine finds depiction. With Pre-Axis, the feminine's primary manifestation was the primordial mother, the mother as source. Now we begin to find additional forms whose chthonic potency can evoke very different feelings. One example is the "death mother" or "terrible mother." We know her in Hindu myth as Kali. As the Vedas say, "All this, whatever exists, is made to share in the sacrifice." Skulls around her neck, corpses beneath her feet, Kali is fire, dancing that life can be renewed. Importantly, while this aspect of the archetypally feminine can manifest with an audacity unsettling to modern sensibilities, it has an acknowledged, even venerated place in Early-Axis cultures. She is regarded simply as part of the primal potency of existence. A faint memory of her can be heard in Shakespeare's reminder that "Nature's bequest gives nothing but doth lend."[8]

While Early-Axis brings clear separation, only rarely as yet do we find polar tendencies significantly at odds. For the most part at this stage, we experience the archetypally masculine and the archetypally feminine as complementary forces. We see this complementarity represented symbolically in the intertwined serpents of the Greek caduceus or the yin and yang of Chinese Taoist philosophy.

We witness similar, largely positive and complementary relationships with nature and with the body during Early-Axis times in culture. While nature then is seen as capable of acting capriciously, she is generally thought of as a generative force. These are times of agriculture's

---

8   In the rituals of Bali, we encounter the death mother in the ferocious and all-powerful Rangda, battling illusion and bringing what is not timely to its demise. In ancient Mexico we meet her as Coatlicue, her body clothed in snakes.

blooming. And while it is now more possible to separate the concepts of self and body, for the most part the body remains something to be celebrated. Indeed, as with the idealization of the body in classical Greek sculpture, and even more explicitly with Tantric belief in the classical East, sexuality and spirituality, rather than being seen as antagonistic forces as would soon be the case, were often viewed as directly linked.

Creative "Perspiration" (Middle-Axis)

In the mother's body man knows the universe. In life he forgets it.

—Jewish saying

Creation's perspiration stage takes the possible into solid form. It galvanizes the conviction, focus, and endurance that concrete manifestation requires. The work progresses by virtue of heart and guts.

Culturally, this stage begins about the time of the emergence of monotheism. In Europe, it first became visible with the appearance of Christianity, continued through the Dark Ages and the late Middle Ages, and culminated with the beginnings of our Modern Age. Over the course of Middle-Axis times, the Early-Axis focus on numinosity and artistry gradually gave way to the elevation of concerns such as honor, might, control, morality, and perseverance.

With Middle-Axis, culture's Upper Pole comes to assume two faces, one more Outer, one more Inner. Each in different ways gives expression to a now more structured kind of authority. In figures such as kings, emperors, and dictators, we see culture's new powers of dominion, the capacity to take control over the politically chaotic and disparate. In the image of the church, and figures such as the Catholic pope, we see symbolized the parallel imperative to keep dominion over the personal below. The teachings of religion are increasingly moral, set in the language of good versus evil and written in scriptures and canons of holy law. The influence of these two Upper Pole manifestations is in the end close to equal. They exist in a relationship that is at once cooperative and also often highly conflicted.

We see related changes in the relationship between Upper Pole and Lower Pole as we move into Middle-Axis. For the first time, the influence of poles is close to balanced. And no longer are they experienced simply as complementary forces—magic interplaying with mystery. The relationship now manifests as a kind of isometric tension—a struggle between at once conspiring and opposing influences.

A creative frame helps makes sense of this new, easily contradictory kind of relationship. Focusing on the vertical, ascent now requires an active pushing away of the Below. While this new, more contentious relationship can initially feel less creative than what it replaces, in fact, when timely, it is pivotal with anything creative. Without this pushing away, the newly created form risks falling back into the immense power of mystery and formlessness.

Feminine symbolism helps flesh out this at once conflicted and ultimately generative picture. We find images at this stage that represent some of the aspects of the feminine that we most cherish. But we also encounter symbols that can evoke markedly negative feelings.

We could call the most acknowledged of the more positive aspects of the feminine at this stage the nurturant or good mother. She is the mother that cradles, the part of us that is supportive and unconditionally caring. Religion represents her with images like the Madonna. She finds more everyday expression in depictions of the peasant farm woman, children all about, loaves of warm bread just emerging from the oven. When someone says, "Now that is a kid only a mother could love," this mother is the part of us that can see the child as nothing but beautiful.

But at the same time, Middle-Axis reality relegates certain faces of the Lower Pole feminine that were seen to have generative roles in previous stages—such as the chthonic mothers of death and passion—increasingly to the demonic. We find an all-loving god of light above juxtaposed with forces of darkness—even evil—below. Darkness and the unformed are more and more often equated with sin.

The ambivalence that can be felt toward the archetypally feminine at this stage in no way reflects some lack of significance. The power of the archetypally feminine diminishes over the course of this stage, but it remains great. We feel ambivalence at this stage because we at once continue to value the feminine deeply and in some way know that if we value it too deeply all that has been gained could be lost.

This recognition is key if we are to interpret Middle-Axis cultural phenomena at all usefully. For example, people in the modern West can assume that the wearing of the hajib or the burqa in certain Middle Eastern societies reflects a dismissing of the feminine. It does reflect a need to distance from the feminine. But the significance of such attire is almost the opposite of dismissing. Set in the context of Middle-Axis times, it reflects an acknowledgment of the feminine's continuing power. As the Middle East becomes more modern, it is understandable that such attire might be questioned. But more traditionally, the protection such attire has provided has been important to the safety of both men and women.

We see a similar kind of ambivalence mirrored in our relationship with nature and with our bodies at this time in culture. Nature's wildness is seen as at once beautiful and something that must be contained if there is to be order and safety. It is the same with the body. When the body is controlled, its power is respected. But when it is not, the body becomes the very face of evil. Where Middle-Axis practices recognize the body, it tends to be in images of ascetic denial.

Given that Middle-Axis dynamics in culture have been responsible for many historical movements with aspects that are not at all pleasant—for example, the Crusades, the Spanish Inquisition, the often brutal tyranny of dictatorships,[9] and often marked oppression and even brutality toward women[10]—it is important to reaffirm the significance of this stage. This stage in both the West and the East is marked by dramatic accomplishments. For example, in the West we find radical validation of rights with the Magna Carta and major architectural achievements from Rome's Colosseum early on in this period to Europe's Gothic cathedrals near its conclusion. In China, this period began with first emperor Qin Shi Huang's consolidation of warring factions and initiation of work on the Great Wall.

---

9 In the modern world, one of the easiest ways to find Middle-Axis cultural dynamics is to note where conflict is common and particularly intractable.

10 The need to push away the feminine has resulted in real and significant harm. The burning of witches in the late Middle Ages (sometimes men but more often women) provides a particularly dramatic example. While we tend to associate witch hunts with 17th century Salem, many thousands of people perceived to be witches were killed in Europe from the 13th century on.

Creative "Finishing and Polishing"(Late-Axis)

 Fourscore and seven years ago our fathers brought forth, on this continent, a new nation, conceived in liberty, and dedicated to the proposition that all men are created equal.
                          —Abraham Lincoln (The Gettysburg Address)

Late-Axis gives new form its finishing touches. It also brings further separation between poles. From formative process's Upper Pole, truth becomes increasingly rational and material, defined in terms of logic and phenomena that can be seen and measured. From formative process's Lower Pole, truth becomes newly personal and subjective—the truth of aesthetics and even whim. From both poles, attention shifts increasingly to refinement and detail.

The tension between poles found with Middle-Axis subsides significantly with Late-Axis. This is in part because separation is sufficiently complete that fears of re-engulfment need no longer be a concern. But it is also because the Upper Pole has now become clearly dominant. The Lower Pole has become a secondary presence, decorative more than something of substance. In the story of civilization, this is the Modern Age, the last 500 years in the West.[11]

Given the degree to which poles now occupy separate worlds, they are best touched on one at a time. Starting with the Above, Late-Axis in culture brings new sophistication to Upper Pole sensibilities. In Middle-Axis, the Above presented an emotion-charged countenance. Now the posture is more measured. With Upper Pole now unquestionably preeminent, we find new confidence in the security of things ascendant, and with this a shift from questions of control to issues of order, detail, and distinction. Concerns such as objectivity, individual rights, scientific advancement, and economic achievement now stand forefront. Real truth is now fully ascendant truth. And ascendant truth now lies in the province of the intellect. Descartes provided the new credo: "I think; therefore I am."

---

11 In much of the world, this stage has come only more recently. For example, with the East it made solid appearance only with the early decades of the twentieth century. Late-Axis sensibilities today have an important role in most all cultural systems.

Lower Pole dynamics similarly become more refined with Late-Axis in culture. But they also evolve in an opposite way to what we see with the Above. The Lower Pole's influence is now small compared to the Upper Pole's might. The aspects of the primordial feminine that remain are relegated to specifically separate realms: feelings to the subjective, the imaginal to the arts. These qualities are valued—sometimes even idealized—but they are also clearly secondary.

We can think of this new relationship in terms of the juxtaposition of heroic and romantic narratives that order Late-Axis belief and aesthetic. The heroic half of the modern age story proclaims that conscious awareness has now prevailed and that it is only a matter of time until we vanquish darkness—now thought of as ignorance—once and for all. The romantic side of the modern age narrative brings a new appreciation for beauty, and with love, renewed belief in connection of a magical sort.

This new kind of relationship—at once a further distancing and a superficial kind of reacknowledgement—is similarly mirrored in our relationships with nature. Nature during Late-Axis times becomes for the first time something we regard primarily as a resource, there to serve human achievement. Very little of its primordial power remains. And at the same time, we find ourselves more likely to find pleasure and even rejuvenation in it, to engage it as "recreation."

And we again find analogous changes in our relationship to—and as—our bodies. Modern age belief distanced us sufficiently from the body as instinct that we could turn and engage the body with "objective" curiosity. Increasingly, we thought about our bodies in purely physical terms—scientifically as anatomy and physiology, more personally as something to feed, clothe, exercise, and occasionally pleasure. Notions like soul or spirit, if considered at all, were thought of as distinct, dropped like chocolate chips into the anatomical cookie. But in all of this, the body also became both a more legitimate subject of study and a more legitimate personal concern—certainly with regard to physical appearance, but also too when it comes to bodily gratification.

It is important to again affirm that this stage in culture is a time of major accomplishment, particularly given how often today we hear critiques of "patriarchy." In the West we saw oral and kingly truths giving way to a personal reality of individuality, achievement, and intellect; a social reality of law, industry, and economics; and mechanistic science's new world of actions and their concomitant reactions. Institutions came to reflect a new appreciation for individual freedom and personal initiative. Governmental forms became representative; religion entertained newly personal and direct relationships with the divine; and economic competition became its own ethic, freeing business from moral constraint.

Along with such heroic accomplishments, we also saw important contributions that came more specifically from romantic sensibilities. The Romantic Era in the West gave fresh emphasis to nature and the artistic. And, of particular pertinence to these reflections, in the world of love, we saw the medieval practice of having marriages determined by families more and more replaced by Romeo-and-Juliet style images of romantic love.

Transition, the Dilemma of Trajectory, and Cultural Maturity's Cognitive Changes

Most people today think of the cultural structures and beliefs of Late-Axis culture as ideals and end points—needing at best only further refinement. We encounter this kind of assumption whatever the cultural form: institutional democracy, contemporary higher education, liberal monotheism, the objectivist/rationalist beliefs and methodologies of the scientific age—or, as we've examined here, modern notions of individuality, gender, and romantic love. But none of these cultural forms are end points, or if they are, our future will not be bright.

I've described how postmodern thought has challenged many of those absolutist beliefs. But I've also proposed that postmodern perspective also necessarily stops short of the kind of understanding needed for times ahead. In the end, it offers nothing to replace what it so insightfully takes away.

If CST's interpretation is correct, what comes next? What I have described thus far hints at further changes ahead. But we need a closer look if our reflections on the future of identity and love are to have sufficient detail. These observations must be brief. This is a topic I've written whole books about.[12] But for our purposes, this limited treatment

---

12 See *Hope and the Future: Confronting Today's Crisis of Purpose* or *Cultural Maturity: A Guidebook for the Future.*

should suffice. Our main interest lies with how more fully understanding today's changes can help us make sense of the challenges ahead for identity and love.

Both the critical need for something more and a glimpse of what more is needed can be understood to follow from the developmental progression I've just presented. We've seen how with Late-Axis dynamics the archetypally masculine increasingly predominates while the archetypally feminine comes to play a secondary, largely decorative role. Postmodern perspective's hyper-rational critiques continue this general trajectory, with the archetypally masculine now becoming in effect the whole of truth and the archetypally feminine for all intents and purposes now out of the picture (witness the techno-utopian thinking that so often defines our time). CST calls this further developmental period Transition.

Transition confronts us with a critical recognition. Further extending what we have seen presents an ultimately untenable situation. CST calls it the Dilemma of Trajectory. Continue on in history's past direction and we would eventually find ourselves severed from aspects of ourselves critical to our humanness.

Using the language I've applied here, we would lose any connection with the archetypally feminine. That means ultimately losing contact with any of the non-rational aspects of intelligence—the feeling parts of us that provide the roots of relationship, the more imaginative aspects that give us art and music, and also primordial sensibilities that provide our connections with nature, with the spiritual, and with bodily experience. Without these dimensions of ourselves, life would come to lack meaning—in the end, to lack life. There would be little reason to continue.

We can recognize the Dilemma of Trajectory in current social realities. The unending superficiality of mass material culture has today become a glamorized last refuge for the receptive. And our modern disconnect from intelligence's more primordial sensibilities manifests in particularly graphic ways in our amazing capacity to ignore damage to the environment and the degree to which we have become alienated from our own bodies. I suspect this disconnect plays a major role in the growing prevalence of addiction—addiction to drugs, certainly, but also with our modern obesity epidemic, and how readily today people become addicted to their electronic devices. CST refers to such ultimately untenable dynamics as Transitional Absurdities.[13] A key way such absurdity manifests is in what I call our times' Crisis of Purpose. With growing frequency, people lack a cultural story sufficiently compelling to give their lives meaning.[14]

Cultural Maturity's changes are what offer the possibility of getting past this that could seem a dead-end circumstance. I've described how Cultural Maturity involves not just stepping beyond the past's parental relationship with culture, but also specific cognitive changes. This cognitive reordering makes possible a more encompassing and complete way of being in, and seeing, the world. It produces what I've spoken of metaphorically as more whole-box-of-crayons perspective. CST describes how we witness related, more specifically integrative changes with the mature stages in any human formative process. Its term for where these changes take us, Integrative Meta-perspective, while a mouthful, quite precisely captures the result.

Integrative Meta-perspective involves at once stepping back from and more deeply engaging the whole of our cognitive complexity. We can think of this in terms of intelligence's multiple aspects. With modern age rational/objectivist perspective, the intellect becomes truth with the other aspects of intelligence's rich multiplicity relegated to a secondary, wholly separate, "subjective" realm. Integrative Meta-perspective lets us step back from the whole of intelligence—including the rational. And at once it offers that we might reengage and more deeply appreciate and utilize the various other aspects of intelligence that are ultimately essential to our toolmaking, meaning-making natures.

We can talk about this same outcome equally well in terms of gender archetype. Polarity at its most fundamental juxtaposes the archetypally masculine and the archetypally feminine. Integrative Meta-perspective offers the possibility of more consciously stepping back from both polarity at its most fundamental[15] and all of polarity's time-specific

---

13 See *Cultural Maturity: A Guidebook for the Future*.

14 See *Hope and the Future: Confronting Today's Crisis of Purpose*.

15 In an earlier footnote I used a creative frame to describe polarity at its most fundamental in an even more bare-boned way. In the end, polarity

and situation-specific permutations. It also offers that we might more deeply engage this rich multiplicity.[16]

A couple of specific consequences are key for this inquiry. First, we recognize the possibility of identity that is more systemically conceived and experienced, what I have called Whole-Person identity. And second, in the world of relationship, we see the option of stepping beyond the two-halves-make-a-whole connections of times past and relating more as whole people. In doing Parts Work, these cognitive changes and coming to sit in the Whole-Person chair are two ways of describing the same result.[17]

These further changes represent a dramatic step forward. And as I've suggested, at the same time we can also think of them as common sense. It is a new common sense we are starting to see. As individuals, in multiple ways large and small, we are beginning to experience changes that reflect the greater human completeness this book is about. These are necessarily changes of a two-steps-forward, one-step-back sort. And it is quite possible that we could run from all they ask of us

---

juxtaposes delineation/difference on one hand with unity/connectedness on the other. This recognition can at first be difficult for people to get their minds around. We are used to thinking of the opposites of polarity as representing two kinds of difference. Oneness would seem to reconcile such difference. A creative frame helps us see how any time we identify with oneness we are quite specifically taking sides.

16 These changes allow us to bring more systemic perspective to all kinds of relationships that before now we have thought of in polarized terms—not just male and female, but also mind and body, conscious and unconscious, political left and political right, science and religion, and more. Integrative Meta-perspective also inherently brings with it needed new skills and capacities, those I've noted in this book along with others that will be critical to addressing further challenges before us.

17 In the end, Cultural Maturity's cognitive changes are integrative not just in the here-and-now sense we see with bringing more systemic perspective to how the archetypally masculine and the archetypally feminine relate, but also in time. One result is the kind of historical analysis this chapter has applied. Another is a growing ability to appreciate—and draw on—the archetypally masculine and the archetypally feminine not just as we know them today, but in the very different ways they have taken expression through history.

with at least short-term calamitous consequences. But, increasingly, we should recognize that our human story is an evolutionary story. Eventually, the new skills and ways of thinking described by a needed new chapter in that story should feel like "second nature."

Other Kinds of Historical Perspective

This chapter's historical observations have focused on the evolution of gender archetype rather than the more common practice of documenting behavioral observations such family and kinship structures, gender role expectations, and sexual practices, I have used the approach I have because it has the most to teach us if our interest is the future. But the more familiar kind of observation can also provide useful perspective, and often perspective that ties in useful ways to these more gender archetype–related patterns. A couple of very broad-brushstroke observations are worth noting in this regard.

The first concerns how we find patterns consistent with cultural stages in how people through time have viewed sexuality. In keeping with the deep engagement with bodily reality that comes with Pre-Axis dynamics, we tend to find the greatest comfort with sexuality and greatest openness to diversity in sexuality's expression in tribal cultures. Some examples: The Bugis, an ethnic group in Indonesia, long ago recognized five genders, each with its own attractions. The Waorani, an Amazonian tribe, believe that both men and women should sleep with as many lovers as possible. And the Etoro of Papua New Guinea believe that all men should have a male lover.[18]

With Early-Axis in culture, consistent with how we see just the beginnings of separation from bodily experience, while we may find sexual practices more specifically prescribed, we don't yet see the explicit distancing from the sexual we encounter later on. I've noted, for example, how we often find the sexual and the spiritual celebrated together—as with the erotic imagery commonly found with Eastern temple artistry or ancient Greece's idealization of the human body. The ancient Greeks also not only accepted, but idealized, certain homoerotic relationships.

---

18 These examples are drawn from Dr Janice Zarro Brodman's book *Sex Rules!: Astonishing Sexual Practices and Gender Roles Around the World*. (Janice Zarro Brodman, Mango Publishing, Coral Gables, Florida, 2017.)

With Middle-Axis and the rise of monotheism, we encounter the most rigorous sexual prohibitions. We see this with the strict practices of the European Middle Ages. We also recognize it in contemporary cultures where Middle-Axis dynamics prevail, such as with most countries in the Middle East.

With Late-Axis in culture we find a gradual relaxing of such prohibitions. The new comfort with the body that we find in Renaissance art anticipated this further change. The Victorian era appropriately gets associated with being strait-laced, but throughout Late-Axis times, at least conversation about the sexual became increasingly acceptable.

Another kind of big-picture pattern has direct pertinence to this book's reflections on identity and love. It concerns the "systemic whole" that functionally defines identity.

I've described how with modern times we've tended to associate identity with the individual, while more accurately the determining unit has been the couple (or the nuclear family). The systemic whole that has functionally defined identity has also evolved over cultural time. Before our modern age picture, it was the extended family and village that defined identity. Before that, it was the tribe.

Thinking in terms of systemic wholes in this way has some fascinating implications for how we think about choice. On visiting Swaziland some decades back, I found that people were quick to tell me with pride that their king had over a hundred wives. My understanding of the significance of this statement changed dramatically when I found out that the most important of those wives were chosen not by the king, but by his mother.

This further kind of evolutionary pattern has important implications for the future of identity and relationship. In another way, we see how Whole-Person identity and Whole-Person love as I've described them represent fundamentally new, and fundamentally important, kinds of achievements.

Insights Pertinent to Both Men and Women

Such more behavioral observations have value, but as should now be clear, drawing as we have here on the evolution of gender archetype supports the needed new understanding in particularly informative ways. Below I've listed a handful of observations pertinent to both men and women that follow from this chapter's developmental/evolutionary picture. They help bring together reflections from this and earlier chapters. I will conclude the next chapter by addressing how these and other observations apply more specifically to the particular tasks ahead for men and for women.

In another way we recognize how the feminine is very much a kind of power. These reflections highlight how the feminine's significance is not only equal to the masculine, at certain times in any developmental process—and here specifically in the developmental story of culture—it represents the much greater power. (As should be clear, power as I use the term here refers not so much to positional power, which tends to reflect more the archetypally masculine even when it manifests in a woman, but rather the kinds of values and sensibilities that prevail.)

Stepping back in this way helps clarify why today we witness such dramatic changes in the worlds of human relationship and gender identity. Developmental/evolutionary perspective helps bring temporal detail to the processes that give us today's changes. I've described how important parts of what we witness can be understood in terms of a further extension of modern age beliefs. I've also noted how other aspects can be thought of in terms of postmodern changes. This chapter's observations help fill out my assertion that the aspects that will be most consequential going forward are products of Cultural Maturity's further developmental steps.

Certainly this is the case with love. What we have seen provides support for my earlier claim that Whole-Person relationship makes sense and becomes possible only with Cultural Maturity's more whole-box-of-crayons picture. It also affirms how it might be possible to move beyond basing our ideas about gender on projection. With Cultural Maturity's cognitive reordering, male and female identities each come to reflect all the crayons in the systemic box. When this is the case, we better appreciate how we are more similar than we have assumed before, and also how in important ways we are different.

Earlier I touched on how Cultural Maturity's changes challenge us to rethink not just love and gender, but also traditional notions of what it means to be an individual. Here again we find confirmation.

While Late-Axis culture has been described as the Age of the Individual, developmental/evolutionary perspective makes clear that what we have been capable of in modern times is individuality in only a most limited and partial sense. Arguably what we have witnessed is not individuality at all, at least not in the sense of being whole people capable of Whole-Person relationships with others.[19] Stepping back in this way makes the needed further step understandable and obviously critical. Cultural Maturity's changes make it possible.

This big-picture vantage also brings nuance to our understanding of just why we have before thought about gender as we have. Previously I described how the mythologized projections of times past have had us equate gender with gender archetype and in the process to view gender in polarized terms. This chapter's developmental/evolutionary framework adds needed detail by helping us delineate just what at different times has been projected. The gradual evolution from archetypally feminine to masculine preeminence over the course of history has combined with the different ways the relationship between gender archetypes has manifested at different times—from perceived complementary, to isometric tension, to greater acceptance of the feminine but in a more decorative role—to directly influence both the qualities we have associated with being men and women and how we have perceived the relationship between the sexes.

These big-picture observations also help us avoid misinterpreting what we see. Certainly this is the case with historical observations. I've noted for example how while the wearing of the hajib or the burqa in contemporary Middle Eastern societies is often interpreted by people in the modern West as a dismissing and denigration of the feminine, more

---

19 I've noted how CST refers to this misconception as the Myth of the Individual. In *Cultural Maturity: A Guidebook for the Future*, I describe how we encounter the Myth of the Individual in another way in the belief that modern institutional democracy represents "government by the people." The relationships between leaders and followers in modern times have remained mythologized and parental—in another way a two-halves-make-a-whole kind of relationship. In Cultural Maturity, I propose that the primary task of governmence going forward may be to realize true "government by the people," this in a mature, Whole-Person/Whole-System sense.

accurately it reflects an acknowledgement of feminine power, indeed a depth of such power that is but a faint memory in modern times.

These observations also help us distinguish what the future will require from outcomes that still leave us short. We've seen, for example, how not just the polarized assumptions of times past, but also notions that make men and women the same fail to get us where we need to go. Viewed through a developmental/evolutionary lens, a unisex ideal is a reflection of Transitional (postmodern) dynamics. It is a product of how we experience gender when our connection with bodily experience is at its minimum. One result of Cultural Maturity's deeper engagement with the whole of who we are is that we recognize something at least similar to the normative 60/40 balance that I proposed earlier.

Developmental/evolutionary perspective also challenges us to rethink assumptions that frame circumstances only in terms of blame or victimization. It is undeniable that much in history—and certainly much in the history of gender—has been painful, brutal, and unfair. But we've seen here how thinking of such harm only in terms of malevolence tends to miss the larger picture. We are to blame if we don't effectively confront the challenges that define the tasks of our time. But history's deep patterns are ultimately expressions of who we are. Holding the big picture this generously is difficult for most people, but doing so frees us from traps that get in our way in our efforts to move forward.

For example, I've noted that today we often hear simplistic critiques of "patriarchy." Particularly people of a more liberal bent may view the changes that have come with patriarchy's rise as inherently oppressive and the problem to be solved. Developmental/evolutionary perspective clarifies how the archetypally masculine's ever greater influence through history, whether manifest in values and priorities or the undue influence of men, has been a natural creative product of civilization's rise. This is not at all to suggest that moving beyond patriarchy in this sense is not an important—indeed essential—thing to do. Cultural Maturity's integrative mechanisms engage us in just this task. But miss the larger picture and we ultimately undermine our efforts. When people reduce the cultural task to "fighting patriarchy," in the end they entrench themselves even more deeply in the narrative they claim to be moving beyond.

Such big-picture perspective helps us tie processes that today are reordering gender, identity, and love to broader cultural
changes. References I made to needed changes in our relationships
with our bodies and with nature help fill out what we see. In the end,
we can understand all the changes that come with culturally mature
identity and relationship in terms of a new, more conscious and integrated engagement with the body.[20] Similarly, a future that is at all
healthy and sustainable will require a new, more integrative relationship with the natural world.[21]

Where this chapter's reflections take us also ties to more specific issues in our time. In other writings I've documented how the cognitive
"growing up" these reflections point toward will be necessary if we are
to effectively address any of today's most critical challenges.[22] It will be
required if we are to get beyond the chosen-people/evil-other thinking
that has historically led to war. (Such thinking puts us in ever greater
danger today with increasing globalization and availability of weapons
of mass destruction.) It will also be necessary if we are to effectively
address potentially calamitous environmental dangers such as climate
change and the growing extinction of species. (Effectively addressing
environmental challenges will require that we get beyond our modern age limits-denying narrative and confront the fact that life often
presents very real limits.) And in the face of today's Crisis of Purpose,
it offers the possibility of a compelling narrative that can provide the
guidance needed to take us forward. (Cultural Maturity becomes, in
effect, the only game in town.)

---

20 For this statement to make sense, we need to understand that being
    embodied in the needed more conscious and integrated sense is new, as
    wholly different from times past when body intelligence stood forefront as
    what we've experienced in more recent times when we've often forgotten
    we had bodies at all.

21 Again, this new relationship with nature is wholly different from some re-
    turn to the sensibilities of times past. Rather, we find a new, more mature
    recognition of our place in nature and with this a new appreciation for the
    great responsibility this place confers.

22 See in particular *Hope and the Future: Confronting Today's Crisis of Purpose*
    and *Cultural Maturity: A Guidebook for the Future.*

Here we have seen how this needed new chapter in our human story offers the possibility of more complete ways of understanding identity and love. It also suggests that in times ahead we could see a level of mutual understanding that before now has not been an option.

CHAPTER FIVE

Gifts—and Necessary Curses

Modern age narratives juxtaposed heroic and romantic stories of who we are and how things work. When people begin to become acquainted with Cultural Maturity's new kind of narrative, they are most apt to think of it in terms of the challenge it presents to traditional heroic beliefs (ideas that have their origins in the archetypally masculine half of modern age narrative). This book has done that, but in equal measure it has challenged complementary modern age romantic assumptions (thinking that comes from the archetypally feminine half of modern age narrative).

Heroic narratives offer that any obstacle can be defeated with sufficient effort and intelligence. Romantic narratives promise ultimate fulfillment in connectedness. With each, we again see how Cultural Maturity's changes produce results that can seem paradoxical. In fundamentally challenging heroic beliefs, culturally mature understanding reveals the possibility of even more powerful ways of understanding and acting. And in similarly challenging romantic assumptions, it makes visible the possibility of new depths of connection with oneself, with others, and with larger purpose.

Here I've given particular attention to the rewards and new possibilities that come with stepping beyond the stories of times past. We've seen how Cultural Maturity's changes alter identity and relationship in ways that in potential benefit us immensely. Whole-Person identity offers a deeper and more complex engagement with the whole of who we are. And Whole-Person relationship makes possible engagement with others that is more rich and authentic both because it brings the whole of ourselves to the act of engaging and because it engages another whole person in all of their complexity. Whole-Person identity and relationship make both being ourselves and being with another person more expressly creative—more available to multiplicity and possibility and more complete in all it draws on in our generative natures.

But it is equally important to appreciate the demands that come with thinking and acting in these new ways. Doing so brings necessary curses along with the striking gifts. This chapter examines some of those demands/curses. It also looks at how the challenges each of them presents help highlight the full nature of a corresponding gift. Juxtaposing demands and gifts in this way provides a good way to summarize observations made to this point and bring them together in a more encompassing picture.

I will begin with reflections that have most to do with Whole-Person identity and relationship. I will then turn to recognitions that more specifically concern gender and implications for today's gender- and sexuality-related conversations. With each we find challenges that may take us by surprise.

Uncertainty and Order

With Chapter Three's look at needed new skills and capacities, I briefly noted the importance of learning to better tolerate uncertainty. Uncertainty's newly brazen presence has multiple layers. Teasing them apart helps us better appreciate how making our way in today's uncertainty-permeated landscape becomes possible and also just what it requires of us. In addition, it helps us understand the rewards that potentially accompany taking on uncertainty's new demands.

The most obvious reason uncertainty intrudes is today's loss of cultural guideposts. We've seen how traditional dictates have differed widely depending on the cultural period and place. But I've also emphasized how the beliefs of any period are ordered by generally agreed-upon cultural rules. When it comes to identity and love, that includes clear moral codes, established gender roles, and basic guidelines for dating, marriage, and childrearing. Such rules have served us by providing order and predictability in a world where the amount of uncertainty would otherwise have been more than we could have handled. Set aside traditional guideposts and we have no choice but to confront the uncertainties of identity and love head on.

I've also touched on an essential new source of uncertainty in addressing the role of change. I've described how identity and love in a culturally mature reality must be engaged in ways that are more "exploratory." It is in the nature of exploration that we can't know ahead of time exactly what it will bring.

Uncertainty also comes to more directly intrude as a product of changes in how the world looks through the eyes of culturally mature perspective. Parts Work provides a simple way to recognize this further contribution to uncertainty. When parts are in charge, we get simple-answer, ideological solutions to our questions. From the Whole-Person chair, truth becomes more multifaceted and dynamic, an expression of our multiple-crayons-in-the-box, ultimately creative, systemic natures. Much more frequently, it takes us by surprise.

Not all of today's new uncertainty is specifically a product of Cultural Maturity's changes. For example, what I've spoken of as postmodern or Transitional dynamics are sufficient to explain much of what we see with the loss of traditional guideposts. But both the capacity to make sense of the multilayered, uncertainty-permeated picture I've described and the ability to navigate successfully in its presence requires Cultural Maturity's cognitive reordering.

The need to deal with greater uncertainty can legitimately be thought of as a problem. If the amount of uncertainty is more than we can tolerate, we will run from what identity and relationship ask of us. But there is good news as well as bad. Cultural Maturity's cognitive changes, by helping us better hold the whole of intelligence's creative complexity, make us more able to tolerate uncertainty. And there are other, more particular rewards that come with taking on Cultural Maturity's less easily pinned-down realities.

The most obvious reward is simply that moving beyond established dictates brings with it greater freedom of choice. As important, when we leave behind projections and more directly engage the whole of experience—including its inherent uncertainties—we better see what is actually there. And the fuller complexity we draw on in ourselves when we do means that choice can come from a deeper and more creative kind of discernment. When we step into Cultural Maturity's necessarily more uncertain world, we in fact find identity and relationship that are more powerful, purposeful, and substantive. In important new ways, with Cultural Maturity's changes, uncertainty becomes our friend.

Responsibility and Authority

I've also previously touched briefly on the need for greater responsibility. Again it helps to think in terms of layers. Certainly if we lack traditional guideposts, decisions come to lie more directly in our hands. But there are also further highly consequential ways in which responsibility becomes newly inescapable with Cultural Maturity's changes.

Earlier I noted—almost offhandedly—how Cultural Maturity's changes make us responsible not just for making good choices, but for determining how we know when a choice is good. In fact, this no small addition. Without culture's parental presence, we become responsible for discerning the measures—the referents—we use to discern whether something matters. This double kind of responsibility presents a magnitude of challenge that before now we could not have fully grasped, much less taken on. The need today to apply newly integrative, whole-box-of-crayons sorts of referents further compounds the challenge.

Whole-Person identity and relationship also make us responsible for making much more nuanced kinds of choices. We become responsible, for example, for asking all the rhythm, boundary, and container questions needed to craft a life that honors both who we are and other people in our lives. Because making such discernments effectively requires Cultural Maturity's cognitive changes, in a further way doing so stretches what we are capable of.

With the previous chapter's historical observations, I made reference to an additional kind of responsibility, one that highlights particularly well the greater maturity that today's new responsibilities require. I described how looking at the big picture helps us get beyond thinking only in terms of blame and victimization. Again, at once we see curses and essential rewards. We confront how the human story has often been far from pretty (or fair). But we also recognize an important sense in which taking responsibility in its larger workings is freeing. At least it makes for more accurate interpretation. Taking such ultimate responsibility also makes for the most effective advocacy. People who see themselves as victims—rightly or wrongly—are also commonly some of the quickest to victimize, a kind of response that undermines any possibility of going forward in ultimately beneficial ways.

I touched on a last, particularly defining kind of responsibility earlier in beginning to address the topic of commitment. It would be easy to think that stepping beyond the clear cultural dictates of times past would make commitment less of a concern. In fact, commitment's demands increase. Certainly it becomes necessary to voice commitments more explicitly—part of the needed clearer articulation of yeses and nos. But we also confront the importance of a deeper and more demanding kind of commitment, both to ourselves and to others in relationship.

Previously, I addressed this especially consequential kind of responsibility by making reference to Parts Work. My commitment to myself becomes that I do everything I can to be sure I make my life choices from that Whole-Person chair. When I fail at this task, I fail myself, fundamentally. Commitment to another person becomes ultimately the same. I commit to making every effort to engage the other person only from that Whole-Person place in myself. My task when I fail is to apologize and also to take responsibility for doing a better job of doing so going forward.

This additional kind of responsibility is no small thing. It ups the demands of life and love considerably. But again, the rewards are similarly great. With regard to identity, the result is a sense of self that is both more rich and full in all it encompasses and more resilient in the face of life's demands. When it comes to love, one reward is commitment we can better count on. Another is the ability to bring greater nuance to our discernments. From that Whole-Person chair, we are able to make better choices.

This last observation, that being committed to Whole-Person perspective results in better choices, is worth some particular attention. Sometimes when love is based on romantic projection, we make very good choices. "Chemistry" can capture a lot in what we need to know. But it is also the case that romantic impulses can leave out much that is important. As they say, "love is blind." The distortions that can come with projection often make us not just blind, but stupid in our pursuit of love.

I'm drawn back to memories of my older sister Jody in growing up. As a young woman, she was unusual in her talents—the soloist in any choir she sang in, a budding opera star. But she was not always so wise in the ways of the world. Through high school and early college, she dated a young man who lived not too far away in the neighborhood.

Carl was fairly average looking, and because he had had polio as a kid, walked with a slight limp. But Jody and Carl were wonderful together, laughing, playing, totally at ease in each other's worlds. And Carl was a good person, loved Jody dearly, and appreciated Jody's unique qualities. I expected that they would eventually raise a family together.

But Jody later met a man who was older, had a fancy car, and was more classically good looking. He swept the young (and naive) diva off her feet. Everyone knew she was making a big mistake (including her outspoken and often annoying little brother), but nothing could dissuade her from marrying him. The (very) short story: He turned out to be a pretty miserable husband and a worse father. Eventually they divorced. Jody died young, and her life was often not a happy one. I've often wondered how differently her life might have unfolded if she had chosen Carl—the more "ordinary" guy who was so obviously good for her.

I suspect that more than just better judgement would have been needed for Jody to have made a different choice, at least more than just better judgement as we tend to think of it. She really needed the ability to get beyond idealized projections, to choose from a more Whole-Person place. If she had had this greater maturity, would she have chosen Carl? I have no idea. But I'm quite confident she would have had a better life.

A couple of further observations are needed if this story is to add usefully to this inquiry. The first is obvious: simply that men are as vulnerable to having the distortions that come with idealized projections get in the way of good decision-making as women. And just as often, the results are not good for men. Given that attractions depicted in the media are almost always of the idealized projection sort, it is remarkable that things go well, for both women and men, as often as they do.

The second pertains to a particularly important implication when it comes to culturally mature relationship, one that can initially be difficult to fully grasp. Ultimately it has great importance. Women and men have historically gained advantage in the courtship game by sending out signals specifically designed to evoke projection (provocative gestures or attire, carefully chosen words). Indeed, we commonly assume that this is exactly what we are supposed to do. People interested in Whole-Person relationship recognize that while such signaling provides short-term competitive advantage, it gets in the way of what they ultimately seek.

This doesn't mean one shouldn't dress in attractive, even sexy ways. And certainly one should put one's best self forward. But people interested in Whole-Person relationship are attentive to those times when what they communicate may be less than truthful, and even if it is truthful, when it may be getting something other than a Whole-Person response. Such attention reflects culturally mature commitment to oneself. It also establishes the needed foundation for culturally mature commitment in relating with another.

It could seem that what I am advocating might take all the fun out of courtship. But when we are coming from a Whole-Person place, it does quite the opposite. It could also seem that this level of sensitivity to what is going on really asks too much. But, in fact, if we are paying attention, the cues needed to tell when relationship is based on projection rather than real connection are not that difficult to recognize.

Confronting these various levels of responsibility can be more than people may wish to take on. But once again, the potential rewards are great. We get more options in life and the ability to love (including loving ourselves) more deeply. We become better able to see clearly amidst life's complexities. And, of greatest ultimate importance, we better own our authority and through this become more fully empowered personally and as social beings.[1]

---

1   It can be easy to abdicate needed new responsibilities even when steps are being made toward greater authority. In her book *Toward a New Psychology of Women*, Jean Baker Miller uses a client by the name of Emily who had made significant strides in therapy toward greater agency in her life—and particularly in her relationships—to illustrate. In Miller's words: "Emily enjoyed acting more honestly and directly 'like herself' and was finding the experience a great new source of energy. She eventually met men who seemed to respond to her 'new self.' But as soon as she became sexually involved with them, she began to lose her sense of herself. 'I can almost physically feel it going. I slip back into an old passive mold. I don't have anything to say about what is happening. It is just happening to me.'" Miller then makes the important addition of tying responsibility's challenge to how we are only beginning to take full ownership in our lives as embodied/sexual beings. "There are several dimensions to this problem. [A key] one involves Emily accepting her own sexuality and allowing herself sexual pleasure. This problem is compounded by old feelings that sex is immoral and dirty. (Such feelings are still very much with us even in these days of

Limits to What We Can Be for Another

Heroic and romantic narratives share all the characteristics I've described for Late-Axis understanding, but one characteristic ties them together in particularly consequential ways. Each denies the fact of real limits. Heroic narratives proclaim that any limit can be conquered. Romantic narratives tell us that finding oneness—with another person or with existence as a whole—transcends limits of every sort. The denial of limits also ties modern age narratives to the beliefs of times past. The stories of each previous stage similarly offered beliefs that protected us from the fact of real limits. Accepting that some limits are real and inviolable takes us a long way toward culturally mature understanding.

The importance of limits that relate to more in-the-world issues, such as environmental limits and limits to the usefulness of beliefs that create a world of allies and enemies, are easiest to understand. But it turns out that identity- and relationship-related limits are in the end just as significant and present just as much of a challenge. I've previously implied a couple of these limits. The need to accept greater uncertainty confronts us with limits to what we can know and predict. And recognizing that romantic dreams of final fulfillment can't be the answer we might hope alerts us to limits inherent in how we have before made our choices.

But an even more fundamental—and easily unsettling—kind of limit steps to the forefront when we engage love more maturely. Whole-Person love confronts us with limits to what we can be for another person (and what they can be for us). The romantic ideal seeks someone who can be our completion. Whole-Person love affirms that there are rich and amazing things we can be for one another, but it also makes clear that being another person's completion is not one of them.

Efforts to escape this limit are in the end doomed to failure. With the early learnings about gender and love that I described in Chapter One, I noted the difficulty I've sometimes felt in giving up the magical hope that there was someone who might know me

---

sexual revolution.) If a woman even unwillingly thinks of sex as bad, then it is sometimes easier to engage in it (to even enjoy it) if she can maintain the concept that it is the man's doing." (Jean Baker Miller, Toward a New Psychology of Women, 1976, Beacon Press, Boston.)

completely. The disagreements of couples who come to see me in therapy commonly have their roots in some version of this difficulty. When I encounter such unwarranted expectations, I often point out that in real life a person is lucky if they understand five percent of themselves. Expecting anything even close to that from another person thus makes very little sense.

Acknowledging that there are limits to what we can be for one another is not easy. We can be left feeling uncomfortably, even desperately, alone. Is the fact of such limits a sad reality? I think ultimately not. But whether it is sad or not really doesn't matter. It is what is true. And it is a reality we pay a high price for ignoring. When we need something to be different from what is true, we inevitably create pain.

Given the magnitude of this challenge, it is important to have ways of understanding that help clarify its significance. Recognizing just how little two-halves-make-a-whole relationship is actually about knowing another person provides a good start. It can also help to understand how much deeper and more resilient (and thus more secure) bonds of a more Whole-Person sort ultimately are. We can also simply recognize that identity and love that can work in our time require this kind of acceptance of real limits. Step back sufficiently and we see that this is all a good thing.

Beyond "Until Death Do Us Part"

One further new relationship-related challenge brings together limits and the need to think more creatively about commitment. Traditional wedding vows include a promise to love "until death do us part." Sometimes today a lifelong bond is the result. And if love remains fulfilling over its course, this can be a beautiful thing.

But like it or not, love relationships in these times of change tend not to be forever. The larger number of people have more than one committed love over the course of their lives. The "until death do us part" aspect of the romantic dream can be particularly difficult to move beyond. We reasonably ask how it might be possible to do so without just replacing hope with cynicism.

The fact that bonds today tend not to be lifelong has multiple causes, but Culturally Mature perspective at least offers that we might hold this fact in more useful ways. Certainly it encourages us to be more realistic and acknowledge that this is another limit that we may need to confront. It also offers that we might reframe love so that our expectations are more appropriate.

One way is to think of love as like a story. Love stories, like all good stories, appropriately have beginnings, middles, and ends. The end of a love story may come with one person's death at the end of a well-lived life. But even with a good love story, right endings can happen sooner.

A person needs to be careful with this kind of reframe. It can be used to justify not making the effort that successful love requires. But it is also the case that letting go of the "until death do us part" narrative can help support the more mature kind of commitment that Whole-Person relationship requires. Our appreciation for our partner can only deepen in knowing that the reason they are with us is always that they really want to be there. And if we can hold all the directions love can go with the needed generosity of perspective, the chance that a love relationship can continue to grow over the course of our lives similarly increases. Paradoxically, the best way to have a relationship endure may be to let go of the demand that it must.

A secondary benefit of leaving the old "until death do us part" story behind is that doing so can make us kinder toward one another should things not go as we had hoped. Earlier I observed how vicious people can be toward someone they have loved when a relationship comes to an end. I noted that this response is a giveaway for the fact that traditional romantic bonds have been based on projection. In order to extract the projected part, the person who we before mythologized and made special must now be made a demon. I also noted that the more common response with Whole-Person love is very different. We will feel grief for the loss. But we also tend to find gratitude for the time we have shared.

A further—and easily unexpected—benefit of this more mature holding of love as narrative is that relationships that end in one form often come to endure in another. One of my closest friends is a woman I was lovers with for over a decade, years back. At one point she shared that trying to be friends, colleagues, and lovers had come to feel like too much for her. We agreed that it would be best if we stopped being lovers. That would not have been my first choice, but I trusted her judgement. Looking back, I think she was right. The more important point is that our friendship endured. And over time it has continued to deepen. I don't think this continued evolution could have happened if we had not each been coming from a generally Whole-Person place in our relationship.

Giving Up Gender-Related Myths

Let's now turn more specifically to gender. Past gender-related myths make a good place to start. If the perspective I've presented is correct, the majority of historical assumptions about gender characteristics have had more to do with projection and polarization than actual difference. What we have seen is a product of culturally defined gender roles and cultural conditioning patterns that follow from the particular ways projection and polarization have manifested at specific previous cultural stages. I'll touch here on some of the more common such polarized assumptions:

Men Are Strong, Women Are Fragile: On average, men are physically stronger, though there are certainly exceptions (I would be no match for Ronda Rousey[2]). But what about emotionally? Historically, by virtue of their traditional roles in the workplace, men have tended to be more comfortable with the rough-and-tumble of in-the-world life. However, with the workplace changing so rapidly over recent decades, this really does not continue to hold up as a generality.

That 60/40 balance means that, on average, men may be more wired for being "thick-skinned." But a good argument can be made that it is ultimately men who are the most fragile. An elementary school teacher friend comments that she finds herself instinctively a bit more protective of the little boys. She senses that there is some basic way in which they are more easily broken. This is consistent with my experience as a therapist. Women tend ultimately to be more resilient, men a bit more brittle.

Certainly women's ability to weather childbirth is remarkable. And there is the provocative fact that women consistently outlive men by three to four years. We can't know for sure just why this is the case, but it is quite possible that the same greater separation between poles that

---

2 A professional fighter, for those who do not stay up on such things.

produces archetypally masculine characteristics also means living life from a more precarious perch.[3]

There are also vulnerabilities that have more specifically to do with role expectations. For example, while the historical expectation that women will assume the more submissive position in relationship might seen to suggest greater vulnerability, in fact taking a Lower Pole posture in relationship can be one of the most reliable ways to establish control and remain safe. The nature of male sexuality also creates a rarely acknowledged added vulnerability. We tend to equate the intensity and immediacy of men's sexual response with power. Certainly it can overpower and in the process leave a woman dangerously vulnerable. But it can result too in men making choices that ultimately do not benefit them. It can also leave men vulnerable to manipulation.

Men Are More Rational; Women Are More Emotional: As a very broad generalization, men tend to be somewhat quicker to draw on rational intelligence as their primary mode for processing information and women to draw a bit more immediately on the emotional. But once again we are dealing with a 60/40 balance, not qualitative differences. Differences within each gender are larger than average differences between genders.

And a further essential distinction becomes obvious with the appreciation for intelligence's multiplicity that comes with culturally mature perspective. The fact that men on average might be quicker to draw on the rational in no way suggests that they are somehow more intelligent. That people could reach this conclusion reflects how we have tended in recent times to equate rational intelligence with intelligence as a whole. In fact, not only does drawing first on the rational not necessarily make one smarter, it can result in the opposite. It can make a person vulnerable to confusing rationalization with truth.

It is important to note that this distinction goes both ways. Because women on average tend to be a bit quicker to draw on emotional processing, people can assume that women are therefore more

---

3 The metaphor of a tree captures both the vertical and the horizontal aspects of this fragility. A tree that is taller, or one that has a shallower root structure, is going to be more vulnerable in a windstorm. And a tree with long branches has limbs can more easily break.

"emotionally intelligent." Women can be. But they can also fall for their own version of the same kind of trap. Reaching first to emotional processing can leave women vulnerable to confusing emotionalizing—emotional reactiveness—with accurate perception.

When it comes to culturally mature intelligence—the ability to sit in that Whole-Person chair, make nuanced discernments, and take responsibility for one's choices—neither men nor woman have any advantage. Men and women may on average go about getting there in slightly different ways, but as far as the needed complexity of perspective, neither gender has a leg up.

Men Are Violent, Women Are Peace Loving: Certainly it has traditionally been men who have gone into battle. It is also true that men commit more violent crimes. But are they inherently more violent? Shortly I will address how, if we define violence more generically—in term of actions that do harm—women can be just as violent as men. Indeed, there are contexts in which they are likely to be more so. But how about the kind of violence that leads to war?

I've heard it suggested that woman are inherently peacekeepers, that by their natures they are opposed to war. But the evidence does not really support this conclusion. It is rare in history that mothers have stood up against having their sons go to war. More commonly the response would be to feel shame if a son failed to serve. The need to protect boundaries is a product of culture as a whole, as is the historical tendency to divide one's world into allies and enemies. In the end, men and women play equal roles in generating the assumptions of the systems of which they are a part—including those we may interpret as violent.

The notion put forward here that we can think of violence as having archetypally masculine and archetypally feminine manifestations helps fill out this picture. Because of the 60/40 balance I've described—and even more because of how in times past we've polarized our understanding of gender—it can be easy to think of women as basically nicer people. When we expand our picture of what constitutes violence, we recognize that men and women are equally capable of being amazing people, and also equally capable of being unpleasant and destructive.

Getting beyond gender-related myths such as these requires that we expand how we usually think. But ultimately doing so serves us, makes our thinking more accurate and useful.

Giving Up Power

I've made brief reference to one of Cultural Maturity's most fascinating and consequential gender-related demands, how it requires both men and women to give up familiar kinds of power. Successful relationship has always required that men and women give up aspects of their gender-based power. Part of love is the tacit agreement by each party to not do harm that each is perfectly capable of perpetrating. But with Cultural Maturity and the possibility of more Whole-Person bounds, this requirement expands. It comes to include not just personal power, but power in more specifically cultural manifestations. It also includes kinds of power closely tied to the old definition of success in love. Again, this requirement presents new challenges. But it also again produces essential rewards.

Men and Power: Because male power is easier to describe, the tasks for men are also easier to delineate. But they nonetheless take us into fundamentally new territory. The first requirement has always been necessary—men have to choose to not use what is generally greater physical strength. This is obviously the case with physical harm. But just as much it pertains to using the potential for such harm to intimidate or create an unequal power relationship.

In our time, men also need to give up kinds of power that follow from ways power relationships between genders have evolved through history but no longer serve us. That includes the assumption up until recently that the "man of the family" appropriately had the last word, and going back in history, that being a husband implicitly or explicitly implied ownership. It also includes giving up past advantages in the workplace that have less to do with the ability to do the job than with the fact of gender. And it means giving up any beliefs men might have that they have a right to venture uninvited into the physical or emotional life of a woman.

I made reference to a final way men need to give up power earlier in proposing that a person interested in Whole-Person relationship will avoid acting in ways that intentionally trigger projections. This means giving up a kind of power that before could be thought of as men's primary initial task with romantic love. In a Whole-Person reality, it is to the great benefit of everyone if men are understood and appreciated for their considerable authentic power. But the culturally mature man knows that mythologized significance, however titillating it can be at least initially, in the end only gets in the way of appreciating the real thing. He can enjoy romantic projections as a kind of shared play, but beyond this he learns to sidestep them.

Women and Power: It is just as much the case that women need to give up power. Certainly in these times when the archetypally masculine rules, women can abuse power in this more traditional sense as much as men, when they get it. But my reference here is to the parallel need to give up key aspects of archetypally feminine power.

Notice that making sense of this importance requires the recognition that women, just by being women, in fact wield immense power when relating to men. The larger portion of this power is emotional. Men have traditionally felt a strong need to have women in their lives. And some of this power is more specifically sexual. Most men are hard-wired to feel considerable attraction to the female body. In each case, this is real power and not to be taken lightly. The culturally mature woman knows such power is never to be misused.

There are also aspects of feminine power that come specifically from the fact that such power is often invisible. The circumstance I described in first introducing gender role expectations, for example, in which men are expected to do the initiating in relationship while often having little idea whether the woman has interest in reciprocating—easily translates into a covert kind of power. The culturally mature woman does her best not to use her power covertly.

The complement to the last kind of power I mentioned for men can be particularly hard for women to surrender. Women have to give up using their feminine cues to evoke projections on the part of men. As with men, in a Whole-Person reality, it is to the great benefit of everyone if women are understood and appreciated for who they actually are. The culturally mature woman rightfully enjoys the delight she can create with her feminine attractiveness. But she also realizes that she does as much harm ultimately to herself as she does to the man if she creates an impression that misrepresents who she in fact is. Women, like men, need to step beyond their past need to attract romantic projections. They too can enjoy such projections as a kind of mutually consenting play if they wish, but they must also learn to set such projections aside when they begin to get in the way of the real thing.

Recognizing When Power Becomes Violence

I've promised to return to the topic of violence for a more detailed look. Previously I spoke of the importance of defining violence more generically, as anything that does harm. Put more in the language of systems, violence becomes anything that does harm to the life of a system. I also described how violence has both archetypally masculine and archetypally feminine forms (each available to both men and women). We gain important insight by breaking this additional observation down further.

Archetypally masculine and archetypally feminine violence each have a variety of more horizontal and more vertical forms (drawing on how I earlier described the workings of gender archetype). Most of what we commonly think of as violence is archetypally masculine violence of the horizontal sort. Here, the life-giving impulse to penetration becomes violation. Physical abuse or sexual abuse reflects this kind of violence. So does gun violence. In some way, a boundary necessary to life—physical or psychological—is not honored, and harm results.

With archetypally masculine violence of the more vertical sort, the generative power of ascent becomes "power over" in a way that specifically does harm. The offending force may be physical control, an institutional structure that limits and constrains, or words that are critical in ways that damage more than they benefit.

Archetypally feminine violence of the horizontal sort invites us in on false pretenses. While it may appear to be receptive, it has the intent ultimately to seduce and manipulate. The implied receptivity may be emotional or sexual. At the extreme, the intent may be not just dishonest gain, but destruction. We know it with images like the "femme fatale."

Archetypally feminine violence of the vertical sort does harm from below. It is passive-aggressive or more overtly undermining. In some way, it keeps life from effectively standing. The person who undermines commonly presents themselves as powerless, but in fact exerts an ultimate kind of control and often does great harm. While archetypally feminine violence of the vertical sort may play out in any kind of relationship, as with the positive aspects of this kind of power, it has its greatest effect with intimacy, parenting, and the family. Carl Jung used the images of the "suffocating mother" and the "tooth mother" to symbolize two particularly destructive forms.

If we frame power in developmental terms, as I did in the previous chapter, violence becomes anything that does damage to our potential as developing beings. Developmental perspective helps clarify my assertion that archetypally feminine violence can at times present the greater danger. The other side of the coin to the fact that at certain times the archetypally feminine has the greater power is that it also at times has the greater potential to do harm.

Culturally mature identity and relationship require that we be more conscious of the multiple forms that violence can take. They also require that we commit ourselves to not perpetrating violence of any sort. In relationship, these various kinds of violence often play one off the other. If we fail to appreciate how violence takes these multiple forms, we can totally miss what is actually going on.[4]

It Is Just All Too Complicated

A lot in the new demands that come with Whole-Person identity and Whole-Person relationship are products of the fact that engaging life with the needed sophistication is just a lot more complicated. I've pointed out the essential paradox that doing so can make things simpler. But it is inescapably the case that with Whole-Person identity and Whole-Person relationship much more needs to be considered.

Most of this book's observations have been of the big-picture, long-term sort. But much of what we have addressed also has direct pertinence to more immediate, front-page-news concerns. I've promised to

---

4 As a therapist, I find that one of the places where this more complex picture becomes particularly striking is when working with instances of physical abuse (most often at the hands of a man). Sometimes the most accurate conclusion is that the man is just a violent person. But rarely are things this simple. More often, particularly if people have stayed together over some time, there is a codependent, it-takes-two-to-tangle interplay of complementary kinds of violence. And now and then, the apparent victim is in fact the greater perpetrator (usually through undermining forms of archetypally feminine violence). A man who lacks the emotional sophistication to respond usefully to behavior that he experiences as violating may lash out in response. Seeing situations this complexly does not make physical abuse any more acceptable. But it does very much affect the approaches I may draw on as a therapist in addressing it.

reflect specifically on contemporary gender- and sexuality-related conversations such as those spawned by the #MeToo movement. Taking
a moment to do so provides a good opportunity to apply some of the
book's reflections to a current issue. It also offers an important example
of the need to take more into account than we might prefer.

In addition, it highlights an important further kind of complexity
that comes part and parcel with culturally mature perspective. When
we apply such perspective to issues that can be politically polarizing, it
takes us beyond the ideological easy answers of both the political left
and the political right. Any time a concern becomes highly contentious—as we've seen recently, for example, with immigration, health
care reform, or climate change—I take time to write an article that
attempts to engage it from a more encompassing vantage.

Previous reflections point toward how a similar effort might be
pertinent to gender- and sexuality-related concerns. For example,
we've seen how thinking more systemically challenges both traditional
notions of clear gender roles (which conservatives might associate with
"family values") and a confusing of equality with equivalence (a kind
of belief more common with liberals). Engaging today's gender- and
sexuality-related debates from a culturally mature perspective should
call into question familiar political correctnesses—of every persuasion.[5]

It has been interesting for me to watch my own responses to the
#MeToo movement and related current efforts. For the most part, I

---

5 In Chapter One, I made the perhaps confusing claim that the roots of polarization with regard to gender and political polarization were related. The
   language of gender archetype in fact provides one of the best ways to understand political ideology. I've heard the U.S. Republican and Democratic
   parties referred to colloquially as the "daddy party" and the "mommy party."
   Think of daddy and mommy in archetypal terms and the description works
   pretty well. CST describes three ways that our thinking can fall short of
   culturally mature understanding, what it calls Unity Fallacies, Separation
   Fallacies, and Compromise Fallacies. Unity Fallacies identity with oneness (we could say with the archetypally feminine), Separation Fallacies
   identify with distinction (we could say the archetypally masculine), and
   Compromise Fallacies split the difference. Liberals tend most often to fall
   for Unity Fallacies (and not surprisingly, more women than men are political liberals). Conservatives tend most often to fall for Separation Fallacies
   (and not surprisingly, more men than women are political conservatives).

see such efforts as very positive. But as I noted earlier, I understand the larger portion of what we have witnessed to this point as having more to do with the modern age project that gave us the Bill of Rights and related equality-related advances in the centuries since than Cultural Maturity's needed further changes. This is not at all to diminish the significance of such efforts—the best in such advocacy continues one of our time's most important directions of social change. And as should be obvious from my observations in these pages, I strongly support prohibitions with regard to sexual exploitation and abuse and see benefit in anything that might engender clearer communication between the sexes.

But it is also the case that I've found much in current efforts disappointing. In particular, I've been concerned to see people's readiness to lump together behaviors and circumstance that should not at all be painted with the same brush. The most obvious lumping together has happened between kinds of implied misconduct in the workplace. Publicized examples have ranged from rape and extreme abuse of power, to unacceptably crass or lewd behavior, to instances where suggested transgressions were minor at best and by all evidence unintentional. And complaints that had nothing to do with workplace power discrepancies, but rather with social relationships and dating, also quickly ended up being tossed into the same pot.

I think it extremely important that accusations are coming to light and that violating behaviors that should have been called out years ago are getting the attention they deserve. It is also extremely important that those who have suffered violation feel confident that their experiences will be taken seriously and that they will not suffer further harm in making them known.

But if needed steps forward are to ultimately serve us, in addition we need to bring much greater sophistication and complexity to how we think about possible wrongdoing and do everything possible to get the evidence required to make needed distinctions. This can be tricky and often not comfortable. It requires that we think with considerable detail about things we might prefer not to think about. And the old "he said/she said" dilemma can be hard to escape.

As part of this needed sophistication, we also need to bring much greater clarity to our communication. The media today often throw out terms like sexual harassment and sexual misconduct with a casualness that implies that what they are describing is obvious. But rarely is it in fact so clear. Given that the ways society should best respond to possible transgressions can be wildly different depending on the specifics, a lack of clarifying detail is no small omission.

Realities are more complex than we might prefer at every level, even when it comes just to workplace misconduct. *New York Times* columnist Froma Harrop emphasized the dangers of workplace overzealousness in a 2018 editorial. She celebrates women coming forward but also counsels that care and perspective are needed in doing so. In her words: "We hear of women going after some schlub in the office because he leered at them or simply asked for a date. An awkwardly placed compliment or a hug would get a guy hauled into the personnel office. These stories have tarnished the #MeToo movement in the eyes of many men—and women, too."[6]

Realities become even more complex when we move into the world of personal relationships. I've described how we are just learning how to say our yeses and nos clearly. I've also suggested that when we step out of the workplace and into the personal sphere, it is often the woman who in fact holds the greater power. Without question it is essential that we more actively prosecute rape and cease to tolerate sexual violation. But it is also essential that we better recognize how poor communication, misunderstandings of intent, and encounters one may regret after the fact are often parts of the messy reality of relations between the sexes.[7]

---

6   Froma Harrop, *New York Times*, June 2018.

7   A group of over 100 French women, including most notably actress Catherine Deneuve, wrote a letter in the pages of the newspaper *Le Monde* that warned of how we can take well-intentioned responses too far and also made an important connection implied in these pages. It began, "As a result of the Weinstein affair, there has been a legitimate realization of the violence women experience, particularly in the workplace, where some men abuse their power. It was necessary. But now this liberation of speech has been turned on its head." It went on, "Rape is a crime. But insistent or clumsy flirting is not a crime, nor is gallantry a chauvinist aggression." The letter concluded by warning of a new, repressive anti-sexuality. I've noted how estranged we can be from bodily experience in our time and

Today's common lack of nuance in our thinking and clarity in our communication most obviously contributes to misunderstanding. But it also gets in the way of the learnings both men and women need if they are to appreciate where lines are appropriately drawn. And it encourages responses that have more to do with ideology than evidence. I've heard it proposed by otherwise intelligent people that since men have been violating women throughout history, a few innocent men getting hurt is not anything that we should be concerned about. Such simple-minded thinking in the end only undermines the support women need and deserve in these times.

I think of this need for greater complexity and clarity in our thinking and communicating as the social equivalent of the need for a more explicit expressing of our yeses and nos at a personal level. It is important that we do a better job socially of asking just what is acceptable and what is not. It is also important that we be more effective in articulating our conclusions.

The systemic view of the evolution of gender and intimacy we've drawn on here supports taking on this more demanding picture. Throughout the book, I've noted complexities that need to be acknowledged if we are to engage today's gender and sexuality conversations with the needed humility. These include how changing social norms can lead to miscommunication, how gender-related expectations of times past were often incompatible with making explicit yeses and nos, how psychological dynamics can alter our perceptions, how big-picture historical perspective challenges us to rethink common beliefs about causality and blame, and how violence is more multifaceted in its manifestations than we tend to assume. Accepting these complexities helps us get beyond both the liberal political correctness often implied with #MeToo advocacy and the like, and polarized reactions to such advocacy that in the end only take us backwards.

Holding realities this large requires bringing greater nuance to today's gender- and sexuality-related conversations than most people are ready for. It also means that not just men, but also women, must confront that they have a lot to learn. But at least making the effort is necessary if potentially important steps forward in our time are to

how much this estrangement exacerbates misunderstanding.

ultimately benefit us. We can be encouraged by the fact that Cultural Maturity's changes support the ability to do so.

Learnings for Men and Learnings for Women

I concluded the previous chapter by listing some of the general learnings we can glean from this book's big-picture evolutionary view. Let's turn now to more specific learnings for men and for women.

Specific Learnings for Men:

1) Equality for women—including equal rights, equal opportunity, and equal pay for equal work—is ultimately a good thing for everyone. Men should be 100 percent behind it. Men should also be 100 percent behind boundaries needed for women to be, and feel, safe, such as prohibitions against abusive language and uninvited touching.[8] Gender-related violation and abuse have no place going forward.

2) Men need to better appreciate the value of archetypally feminine qualities in the world, whether manifest in more sensitive and compassionate leadership, the valuing of negotiation in conflict, or an aesthetic of environmental sustainability. (Note that this is not to claim that women leaders are always more adept on any of these counts.)

3) Men need to better acknowledge the feminine in themselves. That they are becoming more able to do so is a product of a couple of factors. Stepping beyond the polarized perceptions of times past means men become better able to recognize more archetypally feminine aspects that have always been present. And culture's broader reengagement with the archetypally feminine means the archetypally feminine is becoming more available for everyone to engage.

4) At the same time, men need to strongly affirm the masculine. A

---

8   Inherent complexities—such as the fact that what constitutes an "invitation" is not always clear and ways in which past dating assumptions have often invited a lack of clarity—don't diminish the importance of such prohibitions. Ultimately, they highlight the importance of greater commitment to discerning where needed boundaries lie.

common trap is to confuse needed changes with a feminization of men. The men's movement of several decades past—with men sitting around reading Robert Bly poetry—is rightly criticized for promoting this limited and limiting interpretation. Cultural Maturity's cognitive changes increase the depth of our engagement with both the masculine and the feminine. The result for men is a more complete kind of masculinity, no less strong in a traditional sense, but also more aware, and through the greater presence of the feminine, less brittle and more resilient.[9]

5) Men, like women, need to take responsibility for acting from the whole of themselves—in Parts Work terms, from the Whole-Person chair. The result with identity is more substantive ways of being. With relationship it is the possibility of both making better choices and of ultimately deeper bonds.

6) Men need to better appreciate ways that the masculine, when misused, can result in harm—and commit to not letting this happen. They also need to better appreciate ways that the feminine (in a woman or in themselves) when misused can do harm—and learn ways to protect themselves from such harm.

7) Men need to be more comfortable with all the diverse ways that being a whole man can manifest—even if it ends up meaning love is with another man or changing gender identification to better match the felt experience.

8) While the kind of big-picture, evolutionary picture I have put forward in this book is not required to make needed changes, men certainly benefit from having such larger perspective. A more encompassing vantage helps make understandable why ways of thinking and acting that before have been generally accepted no longer have a place. It also helps clarify the new skills and capacities that being an effective man and succeeding with relationship today more and more require.

---

9 The teenage son of a client responded to recent reports of acts of sexual misconduct in the news by deciding that he hated men—and thus himself. Fortunately, his mother was far enough along in her own development that she recognized the harmfulness of this reaction.

Specific Learnings for Women:

1) Women need to continue to be advocates for equal rights, equal opportunity, equal pay for equal work, and equal protection from harm.

2) Women need to better acknowledge the masculine in themselves. Postmodern perspective produces this result in a limited sense by creating a picture of unisex equivalence. But Cultural Maturity, by offering that women might step beyond the polarized perceptions of times past, does so in a deeper and more personal way. It helps women consciously recognize and make manifest more archetypally masculine aspects that have in fact always been there. This is key to making possible the clearer articulation of yeses and nos so critical both to women's safety and to the capacity to relate in more straightforward ways.

3) As part of the general deeper engagement with the feminine that comes with Cultural Maturity, women also need to better appreciate the importance of archetypally feminine power and the particular kinds of contributions it makes. When today we advocate for women having equal power, most often we are referring to power of the archetypally masculine sort. The fact that many women in our time are as out of touch with the archetypally feminine in any deep sense as are men is rarely acknowledged.

4) Women need to more consciously appreciate the value of archetypally masculine qualities in the world, whether expressed in culture's manifest forms or in qualities men more traditionally bring to relationships. If they don't, they will undermine themselves in their own development and respond reactively to men in ways that ultimately benefit no one.

5) Women, like men, need to take responsibility for acting from the whole of themselves—in Parts Work terms, from the Whole-Person chair. The result with identity is more substantive ways of being. With relationship it is the possibility of both making better choices and of ultimately deeper bonds.

6) Women need to be more comfortable with all the diverse ways that being a woman can manifest—even if it ends up meaning love is with another woman or changing gender identification to better match the felt experience.

7) Women need to better appreciate ways that the feminine, when misused, can result in harm—and commit to not letting this happen. It is possible to more deeply manifest the archetypally feminine in a positive sense only to the degree one is willing too to acknowledge the destructive ways the archetypally feminine can take expression. Women also need to be more conscious of ways that the masculine (in men and in themselves) when misused can do harm—and take needed steps to protect themselves from such harm.

8) While the kind of big-picture, evolutionary picture I have put forward in this book is not required to make needed changes, women certainly benefit from having such larger perspective. A more encompassing vantage helps clarify the new skills and capacities that being a powerful woman and having successful relationships will more and more require. Of particular importance, culturally mature evolutionary perspective helps make understandable how a distancing, and even a dismissing, of the archetypally feminine has been inherent to the process that has given us civilization's rise. The advocate for women's rights who can frame the past in larger terms than victimization and oppression gains powerful leverage when it comes to being a force for needed changes going forward. Evolutionary perspective also makes understandable how a conscious reengagement with the feminine is critical to our times and the tasks ahead.

CHAPTER SIX

Further Complexity ...
and a Bit More Pattern

We'll turn to a few additional complexity-related topics in wrapping up. Each relates to how context affects how we make choices. These topics will involve more detail than some readers of this book may need. Arguably this chapter is most appropriate for the efforts of people in the helping professions. But the average reader should at least benefit from recognizing that these further kinds of complexity affect their choices. And more conceptually, the underlying patterns I will describe are at least provocative. Recognizing how they come into play in further ways helps turn complexity into possibility—and even simplicity.

The first topic concerns how our choices are going to be different depending on when we make them. We've seen how this is the case as a product of our time in culture. Here we will take a quick look at how this is also true as a function of where we reside in an individual relationship's development. I include this first topic both because it provides an additional tool for making our way in today's more demanding relationship world and because it further highlights CST's power as an approach for making sense of change in human systems. CST alerts us to how we can recognize a related kind of patterning with human developmental processes of all sorts.

The second topic turns more specifically to how we are different from one another. We will look into some of the implications of personality style differences for how we make choices and also for what love today requires of us. In a similar way, I include this second topic both for its practical usefulness and for how it shines a light on CST's ability to address human systems—in this case, more here-and-now systemic relationships.

Both of these further kinds of complexity have always before had a role in our identity- and relationship-related decisions. But as with previous kinds of complexity we have looked at, before now culturally defined behavioral codes have limited their effects. Today's more unfettered and direct engagement of experience means that each now confronts us more immediately. Today's changing realties also mean that in new ways we can draw on understanding these additional kinds of complexity to support the sophistication we bring to our discernments.

Making sense of these observations will again require that we recognize a kind of pattern that we can fully appreciate only with Cultural Maturity's cognitive reordering. Each kind of pattern involves not just complexity in the sense of more factors to consider, but complexity in the more dynamic and creative sense that makes us human. This means that each will require that we stretch how we usually think. But it also means that engaging these further topics offers an additional reward beyond just helping us choose more effectively. Stretching to get our arms around such complexity in turn helps support culturally mature perspective's more encompassing kind of understanding.

More Temporal Context

This book's big-picture conclusions have all involved putting identity and love in a particularly overarching kind of temporal context— the evolution of culture. We've seen how the ways we think about identity and love, and more than this, what creates identity and love as experience, have changed through history in characteristic ways.

We can expand this developmental way of thinking to other kinds of change processes. When we do, we gain important additional tools for making our way in today's ever more complex identity and relationship landscape.

The most obvious further developmental contextual variable is the one I've drawn on metaphorically in speaking of a needed cultural "growing up": individual psychological development. Over the course of our lifetimes, we proceed through identifiable developmental stages. With each stage, not only do our needs change in predictable ways, but how we understand does as well. This includes how we understand identity and love.

Developmental psychology was added to the social sciences only in the last century. Given that today even the most basic study of psychology would be incomplete without an introduction to stages in individual development, this might come as a surprise. CST proposes an explanation. As with cultural stages, we need at least the beginnings of culturally mature perspective to fully grasp how deeply developmental stages in our individual lives alter our experience of reality.

CST also ties these personal and developmental observations together in a way that has radical implications. It describes how stages in individual development in important ways parallel those we've observed for development in culture. Its explanation for such perhaps surprising similarities is that each kind of change is a formative/creative process. Each reflects how such processes work in human systems. (I've described CST's claim that human intelligence is structured specifically to support our tool-making, meaning-making—we could say simply "creative"—natures.)[1]

Shortly I'll touch on how the dynamics of identity and love change as part of individual development. Going into great detail in this regard is beyond our scope in this short book. But simply recognizing that identity and love change in predictable ways over the course of our lives helps us be more aware and sophisticated in our choices.

Given our focus with this book, one additional kind of developmental change process does in fact warrant a closer look. It turns out that relationships too go through creative stages. Recognizing how this is the case when we are in them can be almost impossible—or more accurately, before now it has been nearly impossible. With Cultural Maturity's cognitive reordering, here too we can begin to step back and appreciate that in fact what we are engaged in is a process—and a very particular, specifically creative kind of process.

Below, I've briefly described relationships in terms of creative stages. And just a bit, I've placed these descriptions in the contexts of individual psychological development and the larger evolution of culture. We can learn a lot from observing how these various kinds of developmental processes interplay. For example, it turns out that our experience of shorter developmental processes such as the course of a relationship is influenced by where we reside in the more extended

---

1 See *The Creative Imperative* or *Cultural Maturity: A Guidebook for the Future* for a closer look at these parallels.

developmental realities that they lie within. Just how a developmental stage manifests, and often whether it is available to manifest at all, is affected by its developmental contexts.

Relationships don't necessarily follow these stages precisely—there is individual variation, and one-step-forward/two-steps-back exceptions are common. But the recognition of general pattern gives us another tool for our relationship tool kit.

Pre-Axis in relationship:

The Pre-Axis stage in relationship is primarily a time of internal preparation—for the integration of earlier experiences of relationship, for deepening one's relationship with oneself. It is important that in entering into a new relationship we first somehow make space for it in ourselves. If we fail to do so, the new relationship will only relive what came before. Pre-Axis is a time for doing the internal growing that will let a new relationship be something that is in fact new

Early-Axis in relationship:

Early-Axis dynamics come into play with the first recognitions of attraction. Feelings may at first be barely recognizable. Or they can be dramatically disruptive. Caught in fantasy and images of possibility, we can become "starry-eyed," fall "head over heels."

As with Early-Axis in other kinds of formative processes, this stage in relationship can be at once profound and also a bit crazy. It is a time of risking in a most vulnerable sense. And at once it is a time when it can be easy to confuse the excitement of what might be with more realized relationship. But even our illusions have their place. They compel us to take the next often frightening steps toward real personal closeness, something we might not find the courage to do if we knew the distance that truly remained between fact and fancy.

If relationship is happening within childhood, this may be the only stage that we see. By virtue of the permeability of child reality, such bonds can be quite close. Or they can offer intense feelings when the actual contact has been but a few shared words, or even just gazing from afar. In later life, love relationships can end here, either because there is not enough substance for them to go further or from fear of dealing with the challenges of the next stage. And sometimes development in a relationship stops at this point but the people remain together. If this happens, the relationship becomes ordered around habitual patterns of fantasy.

Middle-Axis in relationship:

With Middle-Axis dynamics, the "honeymoon" draws to a close and we begin dealing with tasks of crafting more substantive relationship. Particularly early on in this, the most emotion-laden stage, we may struggle with discrepancies between our original dreams and the facts of what we discover. Feelings can flip between extremes, sometimes with disorienting rapidity. But eventually we settle into a time of sorting out: working out who takes charge when, risking to express the resentments along with the joys. It is here that we determine whether the relationship is worth working for. And we begin accepting the deep responsibilities that solid relationship necessarily involves.

Within childhood, it is rare for relationships to progress this far. With adolescence, this stage often plays the largest role (and is most commonly where relationships end). Later in life, relationships can stop here either because it becomes clear that there is no reason to go on, or out of fear of moving into the more fully committed reality of the next stage. Relationships that fixate at this stage tend to be either highly controlled or chronically filled with struggle.

Late-Axis in relationship:

By the time a love relationship enters into the Late-Axis stage in its development, there is shared acceptance that the relationship is important and worth committing to. The major groundwork for relationship now established, focus can now shift to the "finishing and polishing" tasks essential for ongoing partnership: more clearly recognizing each person's wants and needs, defining roles and expectations, working out the details of being together. The previous stage's roller-coaster feelings tend now to stabilize as complementary routines are found.

This stage first becomes available in late adolescence and early adulthood, allowing love to move beyond both the dreams and the often-conflicted passions of earlier periods and become more fully established. Again, this stage can also serve as a stopping point in a relationship, either because of good judgement or fear. When growth in a relationship stops here and people stay together, the connection tends to become dry, habitual, and objectified. The partners come more and more to "take each other for granted." More than connection as established behaviors is needed for enduring love.

Integrative stages in a relationship:

As relationship moves past this stage, we begin to confront challenges at a personal level that parallel the more integrative tasks I've described with our time in culture. Within that particular bond, we face the easily disturbing recognition that our past belief that just being with this other person could make us forever safe and happy may have been an illusion. This is a common time for divorce. But if it is right to persist, we find that the reality beyond, while more ordinary than our previous dreams, is in truth a much greater prize. Within the creative process of that relationship, we discover a more authentic ability to in fact love one another.

How encompassing these integrative changes are will be a function of the defining cultural stage. Before today, these integrative dynamics in relationship have always taken place within the contexts of culture's parental presence and the roles and forms of predefined cultural truths. In the future, these changes will increasingly be possible within a similarly transforming cultural reality. It is these more encompassing changes that this book has been about.

Here-and-Now Contextual Relativity: Personality Differences

I've left one of the most provocative kinds of complexity for last—the role of temperament—personality style differences. I hinted at some of its importance early on in observing that, depending on temperament, a man might embody more of the archetypally feminine than a woman and a woman, in a similar way, might embody more of the archetypally masculine.

For this book's reflections, temperament differences gain particular significance for a perhaps surprising reason. Love relationships between people with different personality styles are becoming increasingly common. We've always recognized that in some way, "opposites attract." But in times past, this almost always referred to opposites within the same basic temperament grouping. In the same way that today we are becoming more comfortable with bonds between people of different ethnicities and with same-sex partnerships, we are also becoming more open to connections that span temperament extremes. With growing frequency in working with couples, I encounter relationships between people with different basic personality styles, particularly among those who are beginning to hold identity in more culturally mature ways.

As with the other new complexities I've touched on, these changes do not necessarily make love easier. We reasonably ask why people would choose to take on this even greater challenge. I suspect the reason ties directly to Cultural Maturity's changes. As Cultural Maturity's cognitive reordering makes us more open to our own complexities, it also makes us more open to—and fascinated by—complexities in our worlds.

At the very least, being with someone of different temperament means that we will never be bored. And there is a deeper Cultural Maturity–related explanation. It turns out that the kind of complexity that temperament differences reflect is precisely the kind that Cultural Maturity's cognitive reordering challenges us to get our minds around. In the end, being with someone whose personality style is different from our own makes the relationship not just an ongoing teacher, but a teacher specifically of culturally mature capacities.

To a truly startling degree, people with differing personality styles can seem to live in different worlds. An exercise I've often done in workshops I've led helps highlight just how great these differences can be. I divide people up by basic personality category and then send same-temperament groups off to different rooms. I then give each group a set of questions to answer, ranging from the playful, such as "What do you like to do for fun?" to the very serious, such as "How would you describe your spiritual/religious beliefs" or "What things in life most frighten you?" Groups discuss their answers together. Eventually they return to the main room, and each group shares what it came up with.

My favorite question gets right to the crux of relationship: "How do you know if someone loves you?" One reason I like the love question so much is that the responses given by different groups are often so different. Inevitably, jaws drop. The answers can seem almost opposite. (I'll share a few in a bit.) People are left wondering how it could ever be possible for people of different temperaments to succeed at love.

Given such extreme differences, it might seem puzzling that historically we have largely failed to recognize them. And I'm referring here not just to the average person, but also to people whose effectiveness and contribution would seem to depend on a keen ear for such distinctions, such as teachers and psychologists. I suspect the reason is the same one that makes Whole-Person identity and relationship, and also developmental processes in any deep sense, only now understandable. Appreciating personality style differences, at least with the nuance CST suggests is needed, requires Cultural Maturity's cognitive reordering.

Any kind of temperament framework can be used to begin teasing apart such differences, but CST's approach proves particularly powerful for getting at this depth of difference. The reason is that it engages temperament with the same kind of systemic reach that I drew on earlier in using the language of gender archetype and with teasing apart cultural stages. It draws on the whole of intelligence and applies it in an integrated way.

A Snapshot Look at the Creative Systems Personality Typology
Let's take a briefest of looks at the basic distinctions made by the Creative Systems Personality Typology (CSPT). The typology has a book of its own and an extensive website, if you have further curiosity.[2] Here, our interest lies with getting a basic sense for how an appreciation of temperament differences might support today's needed more complex and nuanced understanding of identity and love. The CSPT uses the same language I applied earlier in speaking of developmental stages.[3] Because we see Pre-Axis patterns primarily with psychopathology, I'll begin here with Early-Axis patterns.

• *Early-Axis patterns:*
Early-Axis patterns reflect a special connection with the inspiration stage of formative process, that period when the buds of new creation

---

2 See *The Power of Diversity: An Introduction to the Creative Systems Personality Typology* or www.CSPThome.org.

3 A unique contribution of CST is that it links more development/change-related observations (what it calls Patterning in Time) and observations that relate to more here-and-now differences such as temperament (what it calls Patterning in Space). The theory proposes that in each case the systemic relationships are creatively ordered.

first make their way into the light of consciousness and the world of the manifest. Earlies often become artists, poets, or musicians; choose to in some way work with young children; or end up making innovative contributions in the sciences or technology. Think Albert Einstein, Georgia O'Keefe, Leonardo da Vinci, or Anais Nin.

• *Middle-Axis patterns:*
    Middle-Axis patterns correspond to the "perspiration" stage in formative process, that period in which new creation struggles into crude, but now solid, manifestation. Middles do much of the hands-on work of society. They might become teachers, ministers, managers, firefighters, physicians, or political leaders. Think Martin Luther King Jr., Mother Teresa, Albert Schweitzer, or Margaret Thatcher.

• *Late-Axis patterns:*
    Late-Axis patterns correspond to the "finishing and polishing" stage in formative process. This can manifest more in a focus on the rational or in giving greatest attention to the more surface aspects of the aesthetic. Lates often become professors, lawyers, or business executives. They may also take roles in the media or the fine arts. Think Barbara Walters, Carl Sagan, Barack Obama, or Martha Graham.

• *Upper and Lower, Inner and Outer Aspects:*
    CST goes on to identify both Upper and Lower, and Inner and Outer expressions of each of these basic personality constellations. These polar aspects draw most strongly on the more archetypally masculine and archetypally feminine aspects of the vertical and horizontal that I touched on in Chapter Two. With my description of Late-Axis patterns, you might have wondered at the juxtaposition of professors and business executives with people in the fine arts. It is with Late-Axis dynamics that we see the greatest distance between poles. Professors and business executives tend to be Late/Uppers; people who pursue the fine arts, and in particular the performing arts, tend to be Late/Lowers.

Conceptual Implications
    Besides giving a feel for just how deeply we can be different from one another, this bare-boned look at CST's framework also supports

important theoretical insights. For example, it helps fill out my earlier claim that, depending on temperament, men can embody more of the archetypally feminine than women, and women can similarly embody more of the archetypally masculine.

Generally speaking, the progression from Early-Axis to Late-Axis takes us from temperaments where the archetypally feminine plays the larger role to temperaments where the archetypally masculine predominates. An Early/Inner man (say someone who is a visual artist) or even more an Early/Lower/Inner man (perhaps a teacher of young children) will embody the archetypally feminine more deeply than the larger portion of Late-Axis women. And a Late/Outer woman (say a television news anchor) or even more a Late/Upper/Outer woman (say a Wall Street broker) is going to embody more of the archetypally masculine than the much larger portion of Early-Axis men.[4]

Returning to my question of "How do you know if someone loves you?" highlights the depth of the differences we find with temperament realities. It also further confirms how much of a stretch choosing to be with someone from a different temperament world can be. The answers given by Lates tend to parallel popular media expectations. (Most people in the media are Lates.) They know their partner loves them when they hear words of endearment, when they receive gifts like flowers or jewelry, and when their partner makes an effort to "look good."

Middles tend to give quite different answers, though because Middles too are affected by media expectations it can take some reflection for them to recognize what they really find most important. Middles tend to value gestures that communicate constancy and evoke a sense of home and family. They want to know that the other person is solidly there for them. That may be simply remembering a birthday. Or it may not be a gesture at all, nor anything that requires words. It may be simply the fact of being there, of being always present in a way a person can count on.

---

4 This book probably could not have been written by anyone but an Early (or if had been, it certainly it would have been written very differently). Being an Early—and an Early with a lot of Lower Pole—for a man I have particularly ready access to archetypally feminine sensibilities. It is also not surprising that I would have an interest in big-picture pattern, and in particular such pattern as it applies to the future. Earlies tend to find particular fascination in discovering interconnections and recognizing possibilities.

Answers commonly given by Earlies can seem almost the opposite of love to Lates and Middles. Earlies often express that they most know another person loves them when their private time is honored and respected. This perhaps mysterious-seeming answer begins to make sense with an understanding of what such honoring signals to the Early. It communicates respect for the creativity that happens in that private time, and with this, that what most matters to the Early is safe in the other's presence. Earlies also often answer that shared laughter is what most deeply tells them they are cared about.

Different kinds of metaphors can work best for highlighting temperament differences with men and with women. For example, car choices make a remarkably good way to tease apart personality differences in men. Lates are most likely to drive cars from luxury brands like Mercedes, Audi, Lexus, or Porsche. Middles tend to own more practical and less showy vehicles such as Chevrolets or Toyotas. They are also most likely to be found driving trucks or minivans. Earlies like vehicles that can get them out in nature (say a Subaru). They also often own old sports cars or cars that one might describe as quirky. If you see a guy driving an old Volkswagen bus, it is almost surely an Early (and even more surely if it is artistically painted or adorned with glued-on plastic ornaments). Cars tend to be much less helpful with women.

A kind of question that I would never have thought of came up spontaneously in a workshop I led some years back. Besides being more particular to women and enjoyably provocative, it was striking because the answers that people with different temperaments gave clearly surprised the people who gave them as much as anyone. It provides good illustration of the deeply unconscious levels at which personality style differences have their origins.

One of the Late/Lower women, while talking about something wholly unrelated, mentioned offhandedly that she budgeted $100 each month for lingerie. The room went silent. A bit defensively, she turned to the other Late-Axis woman in the group and asked, "Well isn't that about right?" and got an affirming response. Again there was silence. The Middles in particular appeared uncomfortable, as they knew what question was likely to come next. One Middle-Axis woman finally said "OK, I'll answer. We Middles prefer basic cotton. Nothing fancy, and certainly nothing expensive." There was then an even longer pause.

Before any of the Earlies responded, one of the Middles quipped, "I don't want to know." The Earlies confirmed that what she was likely imagining was correct. Any time it was an option to do without such attire, that would be best.

This was decades ago, so I'm sure answers would be somewhat different today. Certainly $100 would not begin to suffice for the Lates. But the incident, famous among people who work with CST as the "lingerie conversation," is often referenced to illustrate the depth at which temperament differences work. We tried doing a related comparison with the men around briefs, boxers, and the like, but it didn't help much with making distinctions, nor did it evoke nearly as much interest.

Stories

Let me share some stories. Each helps illustrate how easily communication can go awry when people with different personality styles decide to share their lives. Each also illustrates a somewhat different way people can respond upon realizing the extent of their differences.

The first concerns an incident from early on in the marriage of two close friends and colleagues. He is very much the Middle—a solid, down-to-earth engineer. She is an Early-Axis teacher—more creative, less predictable. They got married fairly late in life. She had three young sons from a previous marriage.

The incident came with their first anniversary. As a present, he bought her a ten-slice toaster. To him, the toaster symbolized how deeply he was there not just for her, but also for the boys. It was a symbol of them together as a family. He felt that he had purchased the perfect gift.

Unfortunately, her response was to feel confused and a bit insulted. As an Early, the present made no sense to her. It said nothing about her as a creative person. And while being romanced was not a great priority for her, it seemed not romantic at all. On seeing her hurt feelings, his feelings ended up just as hurt.

They had an advantage in dealing with the situation, because they were each familiar with personality style differences. Indeed, they first met in one of my classes. They now laugh together about how completely what was meant as a caring gesture failed. I often share the story at personality style workshops as an example of how wholly communication can fail to connect even with the best of intentions.

The second story comes from a couple who I worked with a few years back in therapy. He is a Late/Upper executive at a local television station. She is a Middle/Inner social worker. Their connection was good for the first couple of years of their marriage. They shared a love of travel, traveled well together, and did it often. They came to see me because somehow things had stopped working as they had, at least for her.

In our first session together, she described feeling that he had stopped making the effort to really connect. These feelings confused him. He described doing everything he could think of to make his caring clear. He went out of his way to verbally express his affection, he bought her gifts, he took care with his appearance. He asked her what more he could possibly do.

She took time to reflect before she responded. She described wanting more quiet time together. And she wanted them to do a better job of simply listening to one another. She also wanted him to be more appreciative of her work and all it required of her.

He promised to try to do better. But he also expressed that he wasn't sure he knew how to do the things she was asking of him. After a pause, they then both smiled in recognition. They had realized at once how little of what she was asking for had to do with "trying" or "doing," In fact, what she was asking for was really almost the opposite. She was wanting more listening, more receptivity ... more "not doing."

The ensuing sessions were enlightening for both of them. Talking more explicitly about how their personality styles were different helped each of them begin to better communicate their caring—and be caring in ways that would better work for each of them. As important, appreciating those differences helped them be humble to the fact that neither of them could ever understand the other person's needs as well as they might like. At one point, he admitted that even though he now better understood what she needed, he didn't think he would ever be very good at it.

This admission was significant not just because of its honesty, but also because it forced her to similarly confront herself. In a related way, she often failed to recognize needs in him that were just as important. Accepting that these limitations were part of the price they would need to pay for the ways in which their differences added to their life together helped them find ways to have their relationship not just again grow closer, but also deepen.

I include a third example because it illustrates how an appreciation of personality style differences can just as easily produce results that we might think of as less positive. It again comes from work with a couple in therapy. He is an Early-Axis jazz musician. She is a Late/Lower owner of an art gallery. They had been initially attracted to each other by their shared interest in the arts.

Earlies and Late/Lowers tend to be the two personalities most drawn to artistic expression. But at the same time—often to the surprise of people with these temperaments who decide to become partners—Earlies and Late/Lowers in important ways almost couldn't be more different. Those differences came to a head when this couple began to talk about marriage—or rather, when she began to talk about marriage.

At first he went along, and she began to do the planning—indeed, elaborate planning. Then at one point it became clear that he was dragging his feet. She found this confusing, because they clearly cared about one another. In fact, he found it confusing too. But he had to admit that he was feeling reluctance.

With this recognition, cracks began to form in what had been a good relationship for both of them. Her initial response was to accuse him of being afraid of commitment and to suggest that he see a therapist.

She pretty quickly recognized that her response was not helpful, but neither of them had a good way to make sense of what was happening or a clue what to do about it. Eventually they decided to see a therapist together, which is where I came into the picture.

Just how deeply their temperament differences were playing a role in the confusion quickly became apparent as we worked together. Their shared appreciation for the arts had led them to miss how fundamental their differences were. The topic of marriage had begun to put those differences in relief. We talked at length about these differences and how they might be predicted given their personality styles.

With this deeper understanding of their differences, what they were experiencing began to make more sense. She had assumed that his reaction toward her had come either from a lack of caring or from a fear of really being close. But, in fact, his response had had an almost opposite source.

In one session, he shared that he loved her deeply and would be happy to live the rest of his life with her. He offered that in fact he was quite open to getting married—in time—though he did recognize that this was less important to him than to her. But he also shared how all her talk about the wedding—the church, the flowers, all the planning—rather than having him feel loved, had had him feeling left out and not seen. What mattered to him was the feelings that had grown between them. He described beginning to feel like an object, and an object she didn't really see.

Recognizing these differences in what marriage signified started a deeper conversation between them about differences. In particular, they looked at choices they would need to make if they decided to live their lives together. In doing so, they recognized that often their needs might take them in markedly different directions.

In therapy, we talked about how it was rarely the case that one of the directions they described was right or wrong—each had integrity. We also talked about how this depth of difference was perfectly compatible with a fulfilling long-term bond if each person understood and accepted it. But they had to admit that the differences were stark, more so than either of them had previously realized.

A lot of soul searching followed. Eventually they concluded that precisely because they cared deeply about one another, attempting to create a life together was not the best choice. This conclusion made each of them sad. They shared mutual tears of grief. But I think they each recognized that they were making the most loving decision.

More on Violence

An understanding of temperament differences adds further nuance to previous observations about violence and its more archetypally masculine and feminine manifestations. Archetypally masculine and archetypally feminine violence take different forms depending on the personality axis from which they emanate. I will keep to the briefest of observations, and again, for the sake of simplicity, limit them to dynamics that manifest more vertically.

The progression for Upper Pole violence should make sense from previous descriptions. With Late-Axis, Upper Pole violence (the vertical expression of archetypally masculine violence), simple competitiveness becomes viciousness. With Middle-Axis, Upper Pole violence, order is used to diminish rather than empower. With Early-Axis, Upper Pole violence, the capacity to inspire becomes instead a kind of seductive charisma.

We see a complementary progression for Lower Pole violence (the vertical expression of archetypally feminine violence). Late-Axis, Lower Pole violence manifests as sexual or emotional manipulation. Middle-Axis, Lower Pole violence more specifically undermines and obstructs (like its complement, it is about control, but here control from below). Early-Axis Lower Pole violence does harm by merging or suffocating.

Again these are broad generalities. But even these simple observations can help us protect ourselves from harm and also better avoid inflicting harm. They would help us at any time, but as relationships of all sorts—not just love relationships, but friendships and also business relationship—more and more often bring together people with a diversity of personality styles, such insights take on even greater importance.

A Needed New Common Sense

We've covered more territory than you may have bargained for. These big-picture, long-term reflections have required not just that the reader look into the past in ways many people are not accustomed to, they have also asked us to picture possibilities that many of us may not know in our lifetimes. They've also challenged us to reflect with unusual depth on current circumstances. But if you've gotten this far, I can assume that you have found the overarching perspective—and implied learnings—these reflections have offered at least provocative.

I've described how the changes confronting our experience of gender and of relationships between the sexes today are legitimately confusing, how they directly bring into question much that we have known and often require that we think in new ways. But I've also proposed that these changes are ultimately to be celebrated. I've argued that we are seeing the possibility of understanding—and embodying—both identity and love in deeper and more substantive ways than have before been an option.

I've also addressed important related learnings that follow from engaging this more complete picture of identity and love. Of particular importance, we examined how men and women are not as different as we have before assumed. We looked at how history's familiar polarized picture has been more a product of ways our cognitive processes have before worked than what has actually been the case. We also looked at how the result is no more some opposite conclusion, some unisex ideal. We explored what it might mean to better recognize real similarities and differences, to appreciate both what we share and what ultimately it is not possible to share.

We looked too at how new kinds of skills and capacities are needed if we are to successfully engage the challenges that identity and love today present. Some of the most important included engaging needed truths more directly (and becoming comfortable with the greater uncertainty and responsibility doing so entails), learning to better appreciate life and love as processes, thinking about commitment in more nuanced ways, and more clearly discerning our particular gifts and also ways in which we can do harm. In addressing these needed new skills and capacities, we also examined the changes in ourselves that make them possible and looked at approaches that can support these changes.

In addition, we stepped back and put these changes in the larger context of history. The insights that resulted helped make understandable why our perceptions of gender have taken the different forms that they have at different times. They also offered that we might better appreciate both why we see today's changes and the fact of their major historical significance.

The approach I've used to engage these changes may at times have created its own kind of confusion. In the end, it has involved not just more encompassing ways of understanding identity, love, and history, but a more encompassing way of understanding more generally. My reason for using this approach is that it supports needed clarity in understanding what makes today's gender- and love-related changes of such importance and also what ultimately they ask of us. If I have been successful, it has also helped link these changes to broader changes reordering our lives today that will be necessary to a future we will want to live in.

Beyond a Battle of the Sexes

Might the changes this book has been about bring with them an end to the eternal "battle of the sexes"? As I suggested in the book's preface, certainly not entirely. Much of past conflict has had its roots in needs that are authentically different. And the fact that relationships by their nature bring greater proximity and mutual dependencies means that we can't escape that there will at times be a bumping of heads.

But there are good reasons to think that the kind of conflict we've encountered historically could lessen considerably. The possibility of getting beyond the projections that before have produced polarized interpretations of differences suggests that men and women in the future should at least be able to see each other more accurately. There is also how Whole-Person identity invites a new and deeper kind of mutual acknowledgement. At the least, it helps us appreciate other people, regardless of their gender identification or sexual orientation, more simply as people. It also brings with it the possibility of men finding greater appreciation for the unique qualities that women often bring to the table, and women the reverse.

I've touched briefly on the importance of current gender- and sexuality-related conversations. Might we expect them to support this lessening of conflict? Certainly they are helping us confront topics that for much too long have been swept under the rug. But I've observed too that unless we engage them with the needed sophistication, these conversations could also end up exacerbating the historical battle of the sexes, at least in the short term. We could see a reactive polarization similar to what we witness today in the political realm.

But whatever we see more immediately, if we can successfully take on the kinds of learnings this book has been about, we should in time find a marked lessening of conflict. These learnings make considerable demands. But at the same time, they expand the perspectives of both men and women in ways that could not be more important.

The challenges for men are most obvious. We've seen how men have to give up their past expectations of dominance and any beliefs that justify denigration or violation of women. We've seen too how what is involved requires not just changes in men's attitudes, but changes in how men hold the experience of being a man.

We've also seen how the challenges are just as basic and ultimately transforming for women. Women have to better recognize how they too are capable of behaviors that violate. They also need to get beyond a narrative that sees the past only through a lens of oppression and victimization. Being fully empowered requires it. And being empowered in a way that is capable of deep caring certainly does.

It would be easy to think that these learnings require only that we act with greater awareness or compassion. Here we've seen how awareness and compassion can only be a start. We also need changes in how we think, and ultimately in who we are. When we succeed with these deeper changes, we become better able to see others for who they are. That includes all that we share and all that is unique in each person's makeup and circumstances.

An Awkward In-Between Time

None of these changes are easy. And with all of them we are only taking baby steps. At best, we reside in awkward in-between times. The simple task of questioning past gender stereotypes can for many people be a stretch. The deeper challenge we have looked at here—fundamentally rethinking both identity and love—can be hard simply to make sense of. We are making a start with this deeper challenge in beginning to recognize the importance of more options in the forms that identity and love can take. But what I have described here—engaging a wholly new chapter in the story of identity and love—is necessarily tricky to grasp, and even trickier to fully take on in our lives.

That said, as we've seen, the rewards for even just making a start are immense. We recognize the possibility of deeper and more solid identities as men and as women. We also begin to be capable of more fulfilling intimate connections. And we discover the paradoxical fact that engaging identity and love in needed new ways, while more demanding than what we have known, is also in important ways simpler. We can think of it all as part of a needed new common sense. We are being challenged to live and love from the whole of who we are, as fully embodied beings.

WORDS OF THANKS

The people who have contributed in important ways through the years to the development of Creative Systems Theory are far too numerous to list here. To them I offer a shared thanks. For this particular volume, I wish to offer particular thanks to Lyn Dillman, Larry Hobbs, and Dan Senour for their support in the conversations that led to its writing. I also wish to thank Kathy Krause and Teresa Piddington for their sensitive editorial assistance, Les Campbell for his beautiful work designing the book's interior, and Java Niscala for his striking design of the book's cover.

INDEX

ICD Press is the publishing arm of the Institute for Creative Development. Information about the Institute and other Institute publications can be found on the Institute website www.CreativeSystems.org.

The Institute for Creative Development (ICD) Press
4324 Meridian Ave. N.
Seattle WA 98103
206-526-8562
ICDPressinfo@gmail.com

Made in the USA
Lexington, KY
22 November 2019